SIR THOMAS RICH'S SCHOOL

CW01246217

13,103   TORDOFF   822 TOR

This book is to be returned on or before the last date stamped below.

30.11.99
-1. FEB. 2007

HEINEMANN PLAYS

BILL TORDOFF

Play it Again
Four One-Act Plays

**Notes and questions by
Bill Tordoff**

Heinemann

Heinemann Educational Publishers
Halley Court, Jordan Hill, Oxford OX2 8EJ
a division of Reed Educational & Professional Publishing Ltd

MADRID ATHENS PARIS FLORENCE PRAGUE
PORTSMOUTH NH CHICAGO SÃO PAULO
SINGAPORE TOKYO MELBOURNE AUCKLAND
IBADAN GABORONE JOHANNESBURG MEXICO CITY KAMPALA NAIROBI

Plays and Notes © Bill Tordoff 1996

Music for the songs in *Kaa!* © Paul Woodhouse 1996

Series Editor: Lawrence Till

All rights reserved. No part of this publication may be reproduced, stored in a retrieval system, or transmitted in any form or by any means, electronic, mechanical, photocopying, recording, or otherwise without either the prior written permission of the Publishers or a licence permitting restricted copying in the United Kingdom issued by the Copyright Licensing Agency Ltd, 90 Tottenham Court Road, London W1P 9HE

First published 1996

2000 99 98 97 96
10 9 8 7 6 5 4 3 2 1

ISBN 0 435 233181

Original design by Jeffrey White Creative Associates
Cover design by Aricot Vert Design
Typeset by Books Unlimited
Printed by Clays Ltd, St Ives plc

CAUTION

All rights whatsoever in these plays are strictly reserved and on no account may performances be given unless written permission has been obtained before rehearsals commence from Heinemann Educational Publishers.

CONTENTS

Play it Again – four One-Act plays by Bill Tordoff

Introduction	iv
Josephine and her Sisters and the Amazing Organically Dyed Fashion Collection	1
The Burger Bar	27
The Hole in the Wall	55
Kaa!	83

Questions and Explorations

Keeping Track:

Josephine and her Sisters	114
The Burger Bar	114
The Hole in the Wall	115
Kaa!	115

Explorations:

Activities	116
Drama	118

Glossary

Josephine and her Sisters	120
The Burger Bar	121
The Hole in the Wall	123
Kaa!	124

INTRODUCTION

These four One-Act plays were written for large casts, to give a whole group the chance to share the fun of reading or putting on a play together. Nearly all the parts are characters with individual speeches, as well as lines spoken or chanted with others. I hope you enjoy them.

Although the plays are basically light-hearted, they all touch on serious topics such as authority, women's rights, the environment and the exploitation of minorities. Suggestions for discussion, written work and activities are included at the back of the book.

Bill Tordoff

Josephine and her Sisters and the Amazing Organically Dyed Fashion Collection

Bill Tordoff

List of Characters

Jacob
Narrators
Maids

Jacob's Daughters	**Jacob's Sons**
Deborah	Asher
Dinah	Benjamin, the smallest
Esther	Dan
Hannah	Gad
Josephine	Issachar
Judith	Joseph
Miriam	Judah
Naomi	Levi
Ruth	Naphtali
Sarah	Reuben
Sharon	Simeon
Susannah	Zebulun

Place: Jacob's sheep-farm in Canaan.

Time: Old Testament days.

NOTES

1. Little is needed in the way of a set, but a raised level is useful to provide seating and as a walkway for the fashion show.
2. The script includes two Narrators, but there can be any number, who can be organized as a Chorus to the action.
3. The Maids appear only in the opening scene, and can double up with Esther, Judith, Sarah and Sharon.
4. To simplify reading, some speeches are given to All, though in performance one or two characters will not speak these lines.
5. The clothes in the fashion show are only suggestions. You should feel free to alter both the clothes and the descriptions.
6. The music for 'I Got a Robe' on page 21 can be found on pages 112–113.

JOSEPHINE AND HER SISTERS AND THE AMAZING ORGANICALLY DYED FASHION COLLECTION

Jacob's sheep-farm. Enter Narrators.

Narrator 1 Everyone's heard of Jacob, who lived in Canaan's land.

With a thousand beasts and a dozen sons, he seemed to have things planned.

His favourite son was Joseph: I'm sure you've heard the story

Of how he went to Egypt, where he dreamed his way to glory.

Narrator 2 But the Dreamcoat story's short on facts: one thing it doesn't tell –

Not only did he have twelve boys, but a dozen girls as well!

Narrator 1 The Bible only mentions one, and why's not hard to guess:

A baby boy was a source of joy, but girls count a whole lot less.

Narrator 2 The first few years of married life saw the birth of most of the brothers:

He had taken a pair of sisters to wife, and their maids chipped in with the others.

The bearded Jacob enters and sits. During the following his Maids hurry on and present him with ten bundles to name, whispering a name which he repeats aloud.

Jacob Reuben, Simeon, Levi, Judah, Dan, Naphtali, Gad, Asher, Issachar, Zebulun.

Narrator 2	The tally of sons soon rose to ten, and Jacob had a dream:
Jacob	They'll not just help around the farm: they'll make a football team!
Narrator 1	Another babe is on the way, and Jake's in seventh heaven!
Jacob	Time to pin up the team sheet: I've sired my First Eleven!
Narrator 2	The maid rushed in with the baby, the bonniest that he'd seen.
	She whispered the name and he named it, and the name was …
Jacob	Josephine?? What kind of name is that for a lad?
Narrator 1	And the maid said:
Maid	It's a girl.
Jacob	A girl? You must be mad! I'll try again!
Narrator 2	And try again he did, and said:
Jacob	Now tell me the truth.

The Maid enters with a bundle.

Maid	I'm afraid it's another girl, sir, and this one's name is Ruth.
Narrator 1	But Jacob was set on completing his team, and kept on trying for a boy.
	As each bundle appeared he'd say:
Jacob	Tell me the truth!
Narrator 2	And the answer came:
Maid	No joy!
Narrator 1	There was Deborah and Dinah and Esther and Judith and Hannah.

A Maid rushes on with another bundle. Jacob tears off layers of wrappings and stares at the tiny baby revealed.

Josephine and her Sisters

Maid This one could be a winner, sir! Look: it's little Ben!

Jacob He's far too small to kick a ball: I'll have to try again!

Narrator 2 There was Sarah and Sharon and Naomi, Miriam, Susannah, but finally ...

There is a fanfare. The Maid rushes on with a bundle.

Maid It's Joseph!

Jacob Joseph! At last!

Of all my boys he is the cream,
'Cause he's made up my football team!
Yes, Joseph is the favourite son:
He'll play in goal at Number One.

Maid But what about little Benjamin? Can't he be one of the club?

Jacob He's too small to hold a regular place: he'll have to settle for sub.

Exit Jacob and Maid.

Narrator 1 The boys grew up and helped their Dad to herd and shear his flocks.

The girls could comb and card and full and dye and spin and weave the wool and knit it into socks.

Narrator 2 And then that magic day arrived as glimpsed in Jacob's dream

When the lads at last were old enough to form a football team.

He made his daughters work like slaves, sewing shirts and shorts,

While he sold the exclusive story to 'The Canaan Sunday Sports'.

Narrator 1 (One shirt was far superior compared to all the others,

And the girls were sworn they wouldn't
tell this secret to their brothers ♪

Exit Narrators. During the following the Girls enter wearing long black dresses and line up. Then Jacob trots on carrying a camera, followed by all the Boys (except Joseph and Ben) in soccer kit. They line up while the Girls dutifully applaud. A fanfare sounds and Ben enters with a ball. His shirt says Mascot.

Girls Here's our favourite: little Ben!

Jacob Peace! Let the trumpets sound again!

The fanfare sounds again and Joseph enters wearing a multi-coloured, sparkling goalkeeper's jersey. Taped applause and shouts of 'Joseph!' He turns like a model, then Jacob embraces him.

Jacob That's my boy! A wonderful shirt for my pride and joy!

Now take your place, my favourite son, where you belong: at Number One!

Joseph takes his place in the centre, pushing Ben aside. Jacob takes their picture.

Jacob Next month you're playing an opener, 'gainst the pride of the Ishmeelite nation,

And tomorrow's the start of your training, but tonight: the celebration!

Jacob leaves the stage surrounded by the cheering Boys. The Girls droop and sigh, Ruth, Sarah and Sharon standing slightly apart.

Naomi I don't care if I never see another football shirt as long as I live!

Miriam Same here. I'm nearly cross-eyed with sewing.

Ruth I think we should praise the Lord that we finished them on time.

Sarah and Sharon Praise the Lord!

All	(*mechanically*) Praise the Lord.
Josephine	Why should we praise him for having to work all night? I call it slavery.
Susannah	Hear, hear! That shirt of Joseph's took nearly as long as all the others put together. And what thanks do we get? None!
Ruth	Women have no right to expect thanks just for doing their duty.
Sarah	No, we don't thank the sheep for giving us their wool, do we?
All	No, we don't.
Sharon	And we don't thank the wind for blowing.
Ruth	And we don't thank the lilies of the field for showing us their wondrous beauty, do we?
All	No, we don't.
Josephine	'Course we don't: 'cause they don't work at it! But we don't just happen to sit up all night stitching our fingers together till they bleed! We do it because we'd be beaten if we didn't!
Hannah	Stop whingeing, Josie: it won't make anything any better, and it only makes you go red.
Josephine	Oh, no, it doesn't!
All	Oh, yes, it does!

Esther combs her hair.

Esther	And you'll never get a husband if you're not pretty.

Judith looks in a mirror.

Judith	No, you won't.
Josephine	See if I care.
All	(*shocked*) Ooh, Josephine!

Enter Asher.

Asher	Father says when are you girls going to stop lazing around and feed us? We're starving.

Ruth	Tell him we're coming!
Sarah and Sharon	Hurry, sisters!
Asher	Move, move, move, move, move!

All the Girls except Josephine and Susannah hurry out chattering.

Asher	Jump to it, you two, or I'll tell Father!
Josephine	You do, and we'll tell him who you were with last night.
Asher	How do you know?
Josephine	Never you mind. Off you go!
Asher	Just you wait!
Josephine	And you, Sunshine.

Exit Asher.

Susannah	Who *was* he with last night?
Josephine	I've no idea!

Both laugh loudly.

Jacob speaks offstage.

Jacob	Josephine! Susannah! What's that noise?
Josephine and Susannah	Nothing, Father Jacob! We're coming!

They hurry off giggling. Enter Narrators.

Narrator 1	Football now was Jacob's life: nothing else mattered to him
	As he trained his boys on the practice pitch or worked them out in the gym.
Narrator 2	In the afternoons they had a rest, so the sisters had to be quiet
	As they pressed their kit or cooked the steaks for their special champions' diet.

Narrator 1	But when the sisters tried to rest they'd hear the clang of a bell,
	And a deafening noise from eleven boys as they worked on their pre-match yell.

Exit Narrators. A bell sounds and Jacob and the Boys run on in their kit followed by Deborah and Dinah, still in black dresses.

Jacob	Stand easy, lads! Joseph, you look brilliant.

Joseph is not as bright as his Dad thinks!

Joseph	I know I do, Dad.
Jacob	Had any good dreams lately, son?
Joseph	I dreamed we won and I went on to higher things.
Jacob	That's my boy! Now lads, you're Canaan United: a team to be proud of, and you're leaving now for your first match against the Ishmeelite Wanderers, so let's hear your yell! Girls!
Deborah and Dinah	A-one, a-two, a-three!

Zing, Zing, Zing

The Boys chant with gestures, led by the two Girls.

> Zing, zing, zing, we're Canaan!
> Other teams move over!
> Hear the roar when we shoot and score!
> Our leader is Jehovah!
>
> Other teams are custard creams:
> They don't know how to play.
> They're dead losses: we're the bosses:
> Canaan rules! OK! OK!

Jacob shakes the Boys' hands.

Jacob   Well done! I wish I could come with you, but I have to stay and tend the sheep and the girls. Deborah and Dinah are coming to support you: look after them. You have a brilliant captain and I know he'll keep a clean sheet in goal. Good luck, lads.

Boys   Thanks, Dad. 'Bye!

All run off except Joseph and Jacob who follow slowly, talking.

Joseph   I've got a problem, Dad.

Jacob   You're not injured, are you, Joseph?

Joseph   No, but I don't like diving for the ball: it dirties my new jersey.

Jacob   The girls can wash it: that's what God sent them for. Just one thing: don't sing any of your solos during the game.

Joseph   But I've a wonderful singing voice, Dad: you keep telling me.

Jacob   Wait till the match is over, son. I'll be praying for you.

Joseph   Thanks, Dad. See you.

Joseph runs off. Jacob shakes his head and follows. Enter Miriam and Naomi carrying spindles, each with bright wool.

Miriam   You know who we're spinning this for?

She points offstage.

Father's pet.

Naomi   Aw, not another jersey for Knucklehead?

Miriam   No, worse than a jersey.

Naomi   What, then?

Miriam   A long coat. You know he fancies himself as a singer?

Naomi   Joseph? A singer?

Miriam   Yes, didn't you hear that squealing last night?

Naomi	I thought it was a sheep dying: I nearly sent for the vet.
Miriam	No, that was brother Joe practising his new song: *'I Look Handsome, I Look Smart'*.
Naomi	Well, you can't go by looks, can you?
Miriam	Dad says Joseph needs this coat to make the girls scream on Top of the Pops.
Naomi	You mean, we're making a Screamcoat for him?
Miriam	Something like that.
Naomi	O, Jehovah!

Ruth enters followed by Sarah and Sharon, also carrying spindles with different bright wools.

Ruth	We don't like to hear the Lord's name taken in vain! Do we, sisters?
Sarah and Sharon	No, we don't!
Naomi	Well, I don't like working myself to death in vain, either!
Ruth, Sarah and Sharon	(*Shocked*) Ooh!

The other Girls enter with spindles and bright wool.

Miriam	Do you know who we're making this robe for?
Sarah and Sharon	Yes, for Jehovah God.
Naomi	Oh, you know his size then, do you?
Ruth	No! They mean every piece of work we do is a means of glorifying the All-High.
Miriam	This one isn't: it's a means of glorifying the All-Stupid. It's another fashion number for Brother Joe.
Susannah	And it's going to take four times as much wool as that goalie's jersey, and it'll be a pig to weave.

Sarah	Don't say 'Pig'.
Sharon	Pigs are dirty!
Josephine	That's another thing: that goalie's jersey'll need washing after every game, and not all these wools are colourfast.
Hannah	They'll wash faster than Joseph thinks.
Susannah	Hey, perhaps he'll play so badly that he'll lose his place. Ben's a better goalie.
Josephine	No, it'll take a miracle to change Dad's mind.
Esther	They should have finished the game by now.
Judith	Here's Deborah and Dinah.
Hannah	But no boys! What's gone wrong?

Deborah and Dinah enter arm-in-arm, grinning.

Ruth	Where are the boys?
Deborah and Dinah	Coming.

They burst out laughing.

Hannah	What's so funny?
Sharon	Did they lose?
Deborah and Dinah	No, they won.
Susannah	So how did Joseph play?

Deborah and Dinah look at each other.

Deborah and Dinah	Brilliant!
Deborah	His jersey was brilliant, anyway.
Sarah	What do you mean?
Dinah	You know how bright it is?
Deborah	Well, whenever one of their players got near our goal Joseph started jumping about, and his jersey put 'em off so much that none of 'em could shoot straight.

Josephine and her Sisters

Dinah	And Dan scored in injury time, so our boys won. Then we all joined in the party afterwards. Look at what some of the Ishmeelites gave us.

Deborah and Dinah lift their black skirts to reveal shorter, brighter skirts underneath.

Ruth	Oh, they're disgusting!
Sarah and Sharon	They're sinful!
Naomi	No, they're wonderful!
Deborah	All the Ishmeelite girls are wearing these.
Sharon	Father won't like 'em.
Dinah	Father won't see 'em.
Josephine	Anyway, he'll be over the moon that his team won.
Susannah	Yes, specially when his pet played so well.
Deborah	Shall we tell 'em?
Dinah	They'll have to know. One, two, three.
Deborah and Dinah	They've sold him!
All	Sold who?
Deborah and Dinah	Joseph.
All	Sold Joseph? Why?
Deborah	Well, after the game he was singing about how amazing he is and how he'd won the match on his own, till the others couldn't stand it. So they asked the other team if they wanted to buy him.
Dinah	And the Ishmeelites were seeking a new goalie to help 'em win the league. So they bought him for twenty pieces of silver and they've taken him to Egypt. He dreams of singing there as well.
Deborah	And the best of the joke is they said we could keep his jersey, 'cause it didn't match their colours!

Deborah and Dinah laugh.

Esther	But what are the boys going to tell Father Jacob?
Judith	Ask 'em yourself: here they come.

The boys are heard from offstage.

Boys	We are the champions! We are the champions!

Enter the chanting Boys.

Boys	We are the champions! Hurray, we won!
Josephine	Yes, but you lost Father's pet, didn't you? What will you tell him?
Boys	(*thinking*) Aw. Erm ... Erm ...
Reuben	I know! We'll tell him Joseph was killed in action!
Dan	Yeah! Diving bravely at the feet of the opposing forwards!
Levi	Winning the game for Canaan!
All	Yes! He won the game for Canaan!

Simeon produces the jersey.

Simeon	And his Dream Jersey was all bloodied and torn!
All	Aw!

Enter Jacob. Simeon hands over the jersey and Jacob mourns while All sing.

Go Tell Old Jacob
(*Tune: Go Tell Aunt Rhody*)

All
Go tell old Jacob,
Go tell old Jacob,
Go tell old Jacob
   That brother Joe is dead.

Joseph was a hero,
Joseph was a hero,
Joseph was a hero,
   But he'll not come again.

All follow the mourning Jacob offstage as they sing.

He was United's Number One,
He was United's Number One,
He was United's Number One,
  But not as good as Ben.

Enter Narrators.

Narrator 1 Well, that was the end of United, 'cause Jacob's heart wasn't in it.

He brooded over Joseph's death and grew more depressed by the minute.

The boys took over running the farm as their Father's sight grew misted,

And the years rolled by in Canaan as if Joseph had never existed.

And then there came a year of drought: the rains passed Canaan by.

The corn all shrivelled up and died and the river beds were dry.

Narrator 2 The next year was as bad again, and the long-range forecast dire,

But word came in from Egypt that corn was there for the buyer.

And Jacob said to the brothers: 'Now hasten to Egypt, you ten.

The girls'll have to run the farm with me and little Ben'.

So the boys packed their bags for the journey and their Dad gave them gold in a sack,

Then they disappeared into the sunset.

Enter Girls carrying spindles of black wool.

Narrator 2 And the girls wondered:
Girls Will they come back?

Exit Narrators. The Girls start to spin.

Ruth	Whether they come back or not, there's work to be done. Let's get spinning!
Hannah	What about the sheep?
Susannah	Little Ben's watching 'em.
Deborah	Where's Father Jacob?
Dinah	Lying down.

Josephine throws her spindle down.

Josephine	If I have to spin another ounce of black wool I'll flip my lid!
Ruth	Patience is a virtue, sister Josephine.
All	That's right.
Josephine	What's right about doing the same tedious things day in, day out?
Naomi	Water has to be carried every day, food has to be cooked: we have to work to live.
Josephine	I know that! But spinning black wool every day isn't life: it's death!
Miriam	We have to wear dresses, don't we?
Susannah	She's asking why they have to be black?
Josephine	Thank you! Why not yellow or green or blue or red, like we wove for Joseph? And why not shorter dresses?
Ruth	Because Canaanite women traditionally wear long black dresses.
Josephine	Yes, and Canaanite women are traditionally boring. Which is one reason why none of you have husbands, in case you hadn't noticed.
Esther	We shall get husbands as soon as Father Jacob gives us a dowry. Shan't we, Judith?
Judith	Yes, we shall. Soon.
Hannah	Where are those Ishmeelite dresses, Debbie?
Ruth	I burned them.
All	(*shocked*) Oh, no!

Susannah	They were cheerful! What did you burn 'em for?
Ruth	Father Jacob doesn't want to see us wearing shameful dresses.
Josephine	It's you that's shameful! You didn't burn Joseph's jersey, did you?
Ruth	That's different!
Josephine	Oh yes? Why?
Miriam	Father Jacob!

All resume spinning. Enter Jacob.

Jacob	I thought I heard shouting. My daughters don't raise their voices, do they?
All	No, Father.
Jacob	Esther and Judith, two young men have asked to marry you. Do you want to?
Esther and Judith	Oh, yes please!
Jacob	Oh dear, I thought you might.
Esther	What's wrong, Father?
Jacob	Your brothers have taken all our gold to buy corn. There'll be no dowries for years. I'm sorry.

Exit Jacob. Esther and Judith burst into loud weeping.

Esther and Judith	No dowries!
Josephine	Oh, put a sock in it, you two!
Hannah	Pipe down!
All	Quiet!!

The two quieten down, snuffling.

Esther	Our boyfriends' parents won't let them marry us without dowries: what can we do?
Sarah	Work and pray, sister.
Sharon	Leave it to God.

Ruth	Yes, everything is in the hands of God.
Josephine	You three seem to know all about the hands of God. Been studying 'em, have you?
Ruth	He will provide.
Sarah and Sharon	Yes, he will.
Judith	What if he doesn't provide? Nobody'll want to marry us.
Ruth	Everything is in the hands of …
Josephine	We heard you! But suppose God has his hands full with bigger things, like famines and earthquakes?
Naomi	I say it's our brothers' job to help now Father's getting old. When they get back they'll put the farm on its feet.
All	Hear, hear!
Josephine	Don't fool yourselves. The price of wool's hit a new low, and the bottom's dropped out of the lamb market.
Esther and Judith	(*wailing*) Oh, don't say that!
Josephine	Shut it, you two, and listen! They say God helps them who help themselves, so how about doing something off our own bat for a change?

There is a pause. They all stop work and look at each other.

Miriam	Women helping themselves?
Sarah	I've never heard of that before.
Sharon	No, that's a strange idea.
Ruth	I'm not sure I like it.
Josephine	That's what the angels said when God first made the earth.

She stands up.

I have a plan to make money. Who's with me?

Judith	Will it help us get married?

Josephine	It should do.
Esther	All right. Us two are with you.

Esther and Judith stand.

Hannah	(*standing*) And me.
Josephine	On your feet, unless you want to sit and spin black wool for the rest of your life!

One after another they stand until only Ruth is sitting, spinning.

Deborah	Come on, Ruth: it must be God's will.

Ruth looks round, then stands. All clap, smiling.

Josephine	Bring your spindles and follow me, quick!

The Girls hurry out. Enter Narrators. During the following the Boys and Joseph as a high official with dark glasses and microphone mime the action as it is described.

Narrator 1   Meanwhile the boys were in Egypt.
They'd all arrived totally beat.

They were aching and tired and thirsty
with walking so far in the heat.

Their clothes were all threadbare and
dusty and their sandals were flapping
and worn.

They were shown to a high-up official and
they begged him to sell them some corn.

Narrator 2   At first he appeared reluctant and sat
there just shaking his head

Till they knelt down and cried out 'Please
help us, or else we'll be very soon dead!'

But the secret that none of them realized
as they poured out their story of woe

Was the guy with the mike and the
sunshades was their very own lost
Brother Joe!

Narrator 1	Well, at last he seemed moved by their hardship and gave each a big bulging sack.
	And they paid him and thanked him and psyched themselves up for the weary journey back
	He made Simeon stay as a hostage to ensure that they'd all come again.
Narrator 2	And they promised that next time they dropped by they'd bring along young brother Ben.
	So they set off again towards Canaan on that journey so scorching and long,
Both	And they cheered themselves up as they plodded by singing the following song:

Back Home at the Farmstead
(*Tune: What Shall We Do With A Drunken Sailor?*)

Boys	What shall we do when we get to Canaan?
	What shall we do when we get to Canaan?
	What shall we do when we get to Canaan
	Back home at the farmstead?

            Make our sisters take our shoes off,
            Make our sisters bathe our tootsies,
            Make our sisters weave new outfits,
                Back home at the farmstead.

            Make our sisters pile our plates up,
            Make our sisters fill our glasses,
            Make our sisters work like asses
                Back home at the farmstead.

The Boys march out repeating the first verse.

Narrator 1	But a new word had entered the farmstead as the brothers trudged back from the Nile.

Narrator 2 And the word was diversification. And that means to branch out: in style!

Exit Narrators. Enter the Girls carrying spindles of bright wools, and Ben with a basket containing spindles of black wool. They sing as they spin, the song building in volume.

Song: I Got a Robe

Girls I got a robe, you got a robe,
All of God's children got a robe;
When I get to Heaven goin' to put on my robe,
And wear it all over God's Heaven,
Heaven, Heaven ...

Ben Father Jacob!

Ben hurries down the line with his basket. Still singing, the Girls put in their coloured spindles and take a black one.

Girls Ev'rybody talkin' 'bout Heav'n ain't goin' there,
Heaven, Heaven, goin' to wear it all over God's heaven.

Ben scurries out. Enter Jacob.

Jacob Good morning, daughters.
Girls Good morning, Father Jacob.
Jacob What were you singing, Josephine?
Josephine A song of praise, Father.
Jacob I'm glad to see you all keeping out of mischief.
Girls Yes, Father Jacob.

Exit Jacob. Enter Narrators. The Girls nod at each other and go out during the following.

Narrator 1	Nearer and nearer trudged the boys each hot and dusty day. And they dreamed of their sisters serving them in the most luxurious way.
	They would bring them their meals and fan them as they lay and drank at their ease.
	(What's the use of having women around if they don't do as you please?)
Narrator 2	But little did they know! Oh, little did they know
	Of the plan that was a-hatching in the brain of Sister Jo.

Fanfare. Ben and Jacob bring on a colourful screen and go out. The Boys enter, put down their sacks and look round, smiling in relief.

During the following, the Narrators, Ben and Jacob set up for a fashion show.

Boys	Hey! Home at last!
Reuben	Back at the old farm!

Issachar looks offstage.

Issachar	Look who's been following us!
All	It's Simeon!

Simeon staggers in panting.

Judah	Did you escape from that Egyptian, Simeon?

Simeon shakes his head.

Naphtali	What then?
Simeon	He let me go. Do you know who it is? It's Joseph!
All	(*incredulous*) Go on!
Zebulun	Not big-mouth Joseph!
Narrator 1	Quiet, please! We're nearly ready to go on air.
Gad	Is he staying in Egypt?
Simeon	No, he's coming here. And he wants to sing a new song.

All Oh, no! Anything but that!

Narrator 1 Quiet! Sit down!

Puzzled, the Boys sit. Ben gives a thumbs-up sign and Narrator 2 takes a microphone and addresses the audience.

Narrator 2 Good evening and welcome again to Enterprise Extra. Tonight our cameras are deep in the heart of the Canaan countryside, bringing you the story of a remarkable group of young women, the Jacob sisters. Living on a remote sheep farm, with their brothers away on business and the bottom dropping out of the lamb market, they seemed to be facing disaster. But they refused to give in, and dreamed up a plan to bring life back into the old place, blending traditional skills with modern know-how. Ladies and gentlemen, let's hear it for Josephine and Her Sisters and the Amazing Organically Dyed Fashion Collection!

Applause. Music. As the Narrators speak, each group of Girls appear from behind the screen, display their clothes and go out.

Narrator 1 First, Miriam and Naomi.

Enter Miriam and Naomi in long black traditional dresses which they open to reveal extravagantly modern, bright dresses underneath. They throw their old dresses towards the Boys.

Narrator 1 Since modern fashion ideas hit the old homestead, these two have given the elbow to the traditional black dress. 'If you're young and pretty', they ask, 'why should you look like an old crow?'

Applause. Exit Miriam and Naomi.

Narrator 2 Next we have Deborah and Dinah!

Enter Deborah and Dinah wearing tracksuits and carrying sportsbags. They take off their tracksuits to show their sportswear and produce matching tennis rackets etc. from their bags.

Narrator 2 They're sporting types, but they don't see why a girl can't be both sporty and fashionable. Note that their tracksuits, bags and all their gear are both bright and fully co-ordinated.

Applause. Exit Deborah and Dinah.

Narrator 1 But chief designer Josie knows that some girls still feel more at home in that little black dress. Here are three variations on the traditional theme that she's dreamed up for her sisters Sharon, Ruth and Sarah.

Enter Sharon, Ruth and Sarah in long black cloaks. Each in turn reveals a black dress underneath. Sharon's is long and off the shoulder; Ruth's is short and smart; Sarah's is long and slashed at the side.

Narrator 1 Sharon may be a traditional girl, but she still wants to look her best on that important date. Sister Ruth is off for a day in town, while Sarah is going to make quite an impression with this little number. See what I mean?

Exit Sharon, Ruth and Sarah.

Narrator 2 It can get cold in Canaan when the sun goes down, but whoever freezes it won't be Hannah and Susannah, who intend to stay as warm as proverbial toast in these stylish ethnic outfits which they designed and knitted themselves.

Enter Hannah and Susannah in bright sweaters, bobble hats, very long scarves and mittens. Applause. They swirl their scarves and exit.

Narrator 2 Now the Jacob sisters' chief designer is going to model something that she dreamed up herself to show the fashion world that the girls can out-do the men! Ladies and gentlemen, let's hear it for Josephine and her dreamcoat!

Enter Josephine in her dreamcoat: a wonderful, multicoloured floor-length garment. Applause. She opens it to reveal a slinky catsuit, swirls and exits.

Narrator 1	Every fashion show has to end with a glimpse of what designers are dreaming up for tomorrow's brides. And that's exactly what we're going to see now, because Judith and Esther are getting married tomorrow in these dresses. And Father Jacob tells me that the sisters are providing their own dowries from the proceeds of their fashion business!

A Wedding March sounds. Enter Jacob, with Judith and Esther on each arm clad in unique wedding dresses. Little Ben is their page-boy. He throws confetti. Applause. They wave and exit.

Narrator 2 I'm sure we wish them all the best! Well, our hour's nearly up: just time for these talented young ladies to finish the show with a chorus from their favourite song. A final round of applause, please, for – the Jacob sisters!

Applause. The Girls appear, line up and sing with gestures.

I got a Robe

Girls
I got a robe, you got a robe,
All of God's children got a robe;
When I get to Heaven goin' to put on my robe
And wear it all over God's Heaven,
Heaven, Heaven.
Ev'rybody talkin' 'bout Heav'n ain't goin' there,
Heaven, Heaven, goin' to wear it all over God's Heaven!

The Boys join in the applause and line up, together with the Narrators, Jacob and Ben. They take a curtain call and walk offstage as the (taped) applause continues.

Joseph speaks offstage.

Joseph Hold it! Hold it!

Joseph rushes breathless onto the empty stage wearing a dusty singing outfit, including dark glasses. He takes the microphone. Thin applause.

Joseph Thank you for waiting so long for me, fans! My first song is a brand-new number. I know you're going to love it, and I know it's going straight to the top. It's dedicated to the person I love most in the world, and it's entitled 'Any Dream Will Do'. Take it away!

Music. The curtains start to close.

Joseph Hold it! Hold it! Please! Hold it! No! Hold it! No!

The curtains close

The end

The Burger Bar

Bill Tordoff

List of Characters

English Settlers

Aaron, *the leader*	Faith
Pastor Toogood	Mercy Toogood
Isaac	Verity
Amos	Charity
Job	Hope
Caleb	Daffy

American Indians

Hondo, *the chief*	Rana
Medicine Man	Hona
Zaquo	Mina
Piquo	Diva
Tonto	Mora
Huso	Zera

(Two Indians also act as Narrators. See pages 42–43.)

Place: An American Indian village on the East coast of North America.

Time: About 1630.

THE BURGER BAR

At one side stands a tepee painted with designs including bison. The brightly dressed American Indians are assembled for a ceremony. Hondo wears a chief's headdress, the Medicine Man has a bison-fur headdress.

All We are the folk of the bison:
He is king of plain and hill.
At his step the prairie trembles,
At his roar the earth is still.
His fur is like grass on the prairie,
And great is the strength of his shoulder.
His tail is strong as a snake
And his head is as big as a boulder.

Hondo The bison gives his people all they need:

Men Flesh for meat.

Squaws Blood for drink.

Men Skin for clothes.

Squaws Fat for light.

All Skin for tents.

Men Teeth for necklaces.

Squaws Gut for thread,
Bone for needles.

Men Fur for heads.

The Medicine Man slowly lifts his wand and points offstage.

Medicine Man The bison lets his people take his life.
The chosen one is happy to die.
Call him to his happy journey
To the country in the sky.

Staring fixedly at one spot and raising their hands in supplication, All begin to sing a call very quietly on a high note. As this grows louder Tonto fits an arrow to his bow and aims. The calling fades. All take a deep and audible breath, and a beat after the arrow is released and hits its target All shout 'Yes!' and run cheering in the direction of the arrow. The noise dies away.

Caleb calls from offstage.

Caleb Hello!

Enter Caleb, like all the English Settlers dressed in drab 17th-century clothes. He carries a bundle with large luggage labels saying INDIA. He stops and looks round.

Caleb (*loudly*) Hello! Anybody around?

Daffy calls from offstage.

Daffy Where are you, Caleb?
Caleb (*calling*) Over here, Daffy!

Enter Daffy, his girlfriend, also carrying luggage.

Daffy Is this it, Caleb?
Caleb Yes, this is India, Daffy. Nobody around. It's colder than I thought.

Daffy puts down her luggage.

Daffy I'm just glad to be on dry land. Three months it's taken us from England, hasn't it?

Caleb turns to look.

Caleb Nearly, yes. All the others are off the ship now, *The Mayblossom*.
Daffy What are you looking forward to most, Caleb?
Caleb A good hot meal.
Daffy Me too. I hated the food on the ship. All that salt-pork, and biscuits with weevils. Why did we have to eat them?
Caleb What?

The Burger Bar

Daffy Those weevils. The Captain said 'Some of the biscuits have grubs in, little wriggling weevils, so knock your biscuits on the table to get them out. Then eat 'em'.

Caleb He meant eat the biscuits, Daffy, not the weevils.

Daffy Oh. I thought the other women gave me funny looks.

Caleb Never mind, they say Indian food's hot and tasty. Curry and poppadums and that.

Daffy I can't wait. Let's go help the others.

Caleb Right. Race you!

They run off, leaving their luggage.

Enter Zaquo and Mina carrying heavily laden rawhide bags.

Zaquo We've enough here to feed us for months. I never get tired of bison, do you, Mina?

Mina There must be something different.

Zaquo No! Give me good old-fashioned roast bison every time!

Mina Right, I'll start cooking it.

Zaquo sees the luggage.

Zaquo Wait! Look!

Mina What are they?

Zaquo I don't know.

He approaches them warily and sniffs them.

They're not made from bison.

Mina But everything that humans make comes from bison.

Zaquo They're not made by humans, then. Look: magic writing! Perhaps the Great Spirit sent them!

Mina 'India'. What's that mean?

Zaquo I've no idea. I'll ask the Medicine Man. You make the meal.

Mina enters the tepee. As Zaquo inspects the luggage, a booming gunshot is heard. He looks up, puzzled.

Mina looks out of the tepee.

Mina What's that noise?

Zaquo It sounded like thunder.

Mina But there's no cloud.

Zaquo No. Perhaps it was a tree falling.

Mina There's no wind.

Zaquo No, it's strange.

He points to the bags.

Like these.

Mina Forget it. Come and make up the fire.

They enter the tepee. Isaac runs on followed by Amos, both carrying long guns.

Isaac (*pointing*) See that big one there!

Amos Holy cow!

Isaac That one's a bull.

Amos Whatever it is, they're twice as big as English cattle.

Isaac Here come the others.

Enter the other Settlers, carrying luggage labelled INDIA. Some men carry guns.

Aaron What were you shooting at, men? Indians?

Isaac No, those great beasts, Aaron. See: behind the trees.

All Wow!

Aaron Good heavens!

Amos There's meat there to feed us all.

Pastor God be praised!

All The Lord be praised!

Isaac They ran off when we fired, but we'll sneak up on them. Come on, Amos.

Isaac and Amos run off.

Faith (*sniffing*) Aaron! I can smell something.
Aaron I'm sorry, dear. I haven't had a bath for weeks.
Faith Not you, dear: cooking.

They all sniff rapturously.

All Mmm!
Verity Roast beef!
All (*drooling*) Mmm! Heavenly!
Hope It's coming from this tent thing.
Charity You're right. Look: a picture of a cow.
Hope It's a funny cow.
Charity It's one of those great Indian beasts.
Verity Perhaps this is an Indian restaurant: let's all have a meal!
All Yes!
Charity It hardly looks a high-class place, does it?
Hope Why don't we ask? I'm starving.
Daffy Knock, then.
Hope There's no door, nor knocker.
Job Let's all shout!
Aaron Good idea. A-one, a-two, a-three!
All (*loudly*) The Lord be with you!

They wait, smiling. Nothing happens.

Aaron Again, louder!

They all call very loudly.

All The Lord be with you!

Mina calls loudly from offstage.

Mina Not today, thank you!
All (*annoyed*) Aw!
Job Ring your service bell, Pastor.

Pastor Keep smiling!

The Pastor produces a handbell and rings it. Mina's face appears. She stares, shrieks and disappears.

Faith What a strange woman! Why did she scream?

Pastor She's probably never seen Christians before. Stand back: I'll deal with her.

All stand back except for the Pastor, who rings until Zaquo appears.

Zaquo Do you mind! Who are you and what do you want?

Pastor (*smiling*) The Lord be with you!

Zaquo Who?

Pastor The Lord above. Our Heavenly Father.

Zaquo Oh, right. You're from the Great Spirit, are you?

Pastor Of course not! We're from Great Yarmouth. In England.

Zaquo Never heard of it. Can you wait? We're just eating.

Pastor I shan't keep you. Have your people been here long?

Zaquo About a thousand years. What about you?

Pastor We've just arrived. Do you agree that the search for lasting peace is the most serious problem in the world today?

Zaquo (*peering*) What's wrong with your face?

Pastor Everywhere we read of war and crimes: burglary, mugging, stealing horses ...

Zaquo Horses? What are they?

Pastor They're animals.

Zaquo How do you cook them?

Aaron steps forward.

Aaron Don't be barbaric! No true Englishman would eat a horse!

Zaquo You as well!

He sees the others.

The Burger Bar

All of you! What's wrong with your faces?

All inspect each other's faces.

Zaquo Are you lepers?

Mercy Of course we're not leopards! Leopards are animals with spots! We're human, like you.

Faith We are all made in the image of God.

Zaquo Who's God?

All (*shocked*) Ooh!

Pastor You've never heard of God?

Zaquo Not till the squaw there mentioned it.

Daffy What's a squaw?

Zaquo (*calling*) Mina, can you spare a minute?

Mina appears.

Zaquo This is my squaw. This is our tepee.

He speaks to Mina.

They're travellers.

Mina Why are their faces so pale? Do you paint them?

Hope No, we were born like this.

Mina That's awful! Ask your medicine man for help.

Zaquo Right: don't be embarrassed!

Settlers We're not embarrassed!

Charity This colour is normal for people of our race!

Mina Oh, you're in a race? You'd better keep running or you'll finish last.

Hope When she says race, she means tribe. We're English.

Mina English. And you're not in a race?

Charity These two are fools, and this isn't a café. I'm going to rest.

Others agree and sit on their luggage.

Mina Where are you heading for?

Aaron	We have sailed across the mighty Atlantic Ocean to reach India, fabled land of gold.
Pastor	And silver and jewels.
Verity	And exotic spices to flavour our monotonous diet.
Job	India!
Settlers	India!
Zaquo and Mina	Where?
Job	India. Here.

Mina points to the bags.

Mina	Oh, you brought those! Sorry, you've made a mistake.
Zaquo	Yes, you've got the wrong address. This is America. We've never heard of India, have we?
Mina	No, never.
Aaron	Nonsense!

He produces a map.

This place is clearly marked on the map as India. See! So you two must be Indians.

Zaquo returns the map.

Zaquo	No, someone's sold you a dud map, stranger. We're Americans. Ours is a mixed marriage: my wife here is Cheyenne.
Mercy	Pleased to meet you, Ann. You don't seem shy, if you'll forgive me saying so.
Mina	No, my tribe is Cheyenne! My name's Mina. He's Sioux.
Mercy	Is that his name or his tribe?
Zaquo	My tribe, of course. My name's Zaquo.

Mercy produces a notebook.

Mercy	And how do you spell Cheyenne and Sioux?
Mina	No-one spells us unless they want scalping, sister!
Aaron	Well, whatever you say, we shall call you Indians.

Mercy	Red Indians.
Settlers	Yes! Red Indians!
Zaquo	Well, we shall call you Palefaces.
Verity	And what do you call those great animals over there?
Mina	Those are bison.
Zaquo	If you want to kill one you have to spell it first.
Mina	Yes, you'll never get near enough to use those clubs.

The Settlers laugh.

Amos	These aren't clubs: they're guns!
Isaac	Firesticks. They make a noise like thunder and kill at a hundred paces.

There are two gunshots offstage. Zaquo and Mina look up; the Settlers look in the direction of the shots.

Zaquo	That sound again. Thunder from a clear sky.
Mina	It's the Great Spirit speaking.

The Settlers laugh.

Charity	Stupid! Those are gunshots. Our hunters are coming.

Enter Isaac and Amos.

Verity	Did you kill any?
Isaac	Yes, two.
Aaron	Well done!

The Settlers clap.

Amos	They're a sort of buffalo.
Zaquo	No, they're bison.
Isaac	We say they're buffalo.
Amos	Who do you think you are?
Zaquo	We live here. Why did you kill two? One's enough.
Isaac	Not for us.
Mina	How did you kill them?
Isaac	(*pointing*) You see that squirrel?

He aims and shoots, the Americans yell and cover their ears.

Now you don't!

Zaquo   Amazing. What else can they kill?

Isaac   Birds, vermin, anyone who opposes us.

Pastor   God has given his people dominion over fish and fowl and every living thing that moves upon the earth!

Settlers   (*standing*) Hallelujah!

Pastor   And he will give us all knowledge, so that we shall move mountains!

Settlers   Praise the Lord!

Zaquo   Good! Well, you've a long journey ahead. See you!

Mina   Yes, I've enjoyed our talk. Have a nice day!

Pastor   Wait! God tells me our Promised Land is right here!

Settlers   Hallelujah! Amen!

Mina   Does that mean you're staying?

Aaron   Yes! We shall build a town here, and we shall call it Providence, for we are come by the providence of God.

Settlers   Providence! Amen!

The other Americans enter, including the Medicine Man. The groups stare at each other.

Hondo   What was that noise?

Medicine Man   And who are these?

Zaquo   Palefaces with thunder sticks.

Hondo   (*raising a hand*) How!

Aaron   How? Oh, how did we get here? (*Pointing*) See our ship in the bay!

Americans   (*looking*) Hey!

Hondo   It must take many braves to paddle such a great canoe.

The Settlers laugh.

Rana	Yes, especially with all that washing hung out.
	The Settlers laugh again.
Faith	Those are sails, not washing!
Job	Our ships are moved by wind, if we have the wind.
Huso	If you have wind, hey? What do you live on: beans?
	The Americans laugh.
Aaron	Do not mock the chosen of the Lord! When we have built our town and planted our crops we shall explore this fair land of India!
Americans	Where?
Zaquo	I told 'em!
Americans	India??
Settlers	Yes, India! Here!
Piquo	This is America!
Mina	We told them, but they won't listen!
Isaac	We shall find the gold, the silver, and the spices for which this land is fabled!
Huso	American is a land of great plains, bison, turkey, potato and tobacco!
Hondo	But you're welcome to stay. There is land and food for all, except for the greedy.
Americans	Yes, except the greedy.
Medicine Man	I shall teach you to worship the Great Spirit, and to live according to his law.
Aaron	We have our own law.
Pastor	We fled from England to worship the one true God in our own way.
Settlers	Hallelujah!
Hona	We shall be glad to help you with your farming. This is good land for potato and tobacco.
Verity	Thank you. We look forward to eating them both.
	The Americans laugh.

Hona	You don't actually eat tobacco. Let me tell you …
Aaron	Quiet, woman! Where shall we build our town?

All look round.

Hona	If you ask my opinion …
Aaron	I don't. Men?
Job	That hilltop looks a good place to defend.
Settler Men	Agreed!
Huso	Defend against whom?
Mora	It's a long way to carry water.
Aaron	What do you make your houses from? Brick, stone, wood?
Tonto	We live in wigwams.
Settlers	In what?
Americans	Wigwams!
Daffy	And what's a wimwag, a wamwig, a wagwim, er …
Americans	Wigwam!
Daffy	Yes. What you said. What is one?
Tonto	A wigwam is a tepee.
Daffy	And what's a peetee?
Americans	Tepee!
Daffy	Tepee. Well, what *is* one?
Medicine Man	All the people of the bison make their dwellings from his hide. Like this.

He gestures to the tepee.

Faith	You surely don't live in tents all the year round?
Mora	Yes, even in Winter.
Faith	But we've read that Indians dwell in palaces.
Settlers	That's right!
Hondo	If that's what you want you've come to the wrong place! We're simple folk: we make our clothes and tepees from bison skin …

Rana	We use its sinews for thread ...
Mora	And its fat for candles ...
Zera	We make needles from its bones ...
Huso	And we're happy as the wind that sweeps across the plains!
Tonto	Happy as the wolf that howls to the moon!
Huso	(*loudly*) Happy as the eagle that soars in the sky ...!
Americans	(*loudly*) Happy as the eagle that soars in the sky ...!
Settlers	(*loudly*) All right!! Thank you!
Job	We get the message!
Americans	Sorry we spoke!
Faith	And dare I ask what you eat?
Americans	Bison!
Faith	We might have guessed.
Americans	Yes, you might.
Verity	And what spices do you flavour it with?
Mora	What are spices?

There is a terrible squawking offstage.

Settlers	(*looking*) Aargh! What's that thing?
Tonto	That's a turkey: a flightless bird.
Pastor	But God made all birds to fly.
Medicine Man	Harken to the tale of how the turkey forgot to fly!
Amos	Later. What does it taste like?
Diva	It's not like bison, is it?
Americans	No!
Amos	Why does everything have to taste like bison?
Mora	(*sniffing*) What's that smell?
Mina	Our leg of bison! It's cooked!
Mora	And if yours is ready, so is ours.
Diva	Would you like to share our meal?
Daffy	Ooh, yes, please!

Mercy	No! We shall not trespass on your hospitality. We still have some salt pork and ship's biscuits. Isn't God good to us, Daffy?
Daffy	If you say so, Mercy.
Aaron	We shall eat a Christian meal after blessing the site of our new home.

Aaron speaks to Hondo.

	God go with you.
Hondo	And the Great Spirit go with you.
Rana	Any help you need, just ask.
Pastor	God will provide. Raise your voices to Him as we march!

The Settlers pick up their bags and march out singing.

Settlers
>He who would valiant be
>'Gainst all disaster.
>Let him in constancy
>   Follow the Master.
>There's no discouragement
>Shall make him once relent
>His first avowed intent
>   To be a pilgrim.

The singing fades away.

Zera	Funny folk.
Hona	Well, good luck to 'em: they're going to need it.
Rana	(*sniffing*) Meat burning!
All	Oh, no! Quick!

All run off except for the Narrators.

Narrator 1	The first year on the bleak hilltop was hard for the Palefaces as they cut down the trees to build their wooden tepees. The biggest was for their spirit, whom they call God. He is not like our Great Spirit, who lives in everything.

| | The Burger Bar | **43** |

Narrator 2 Then they felled more trees to clear land for farming, and they tried to hunt with their thundersticks, but they were often hungry. So when the snow covered the prairie we gave them food. And we wondered why they had come with their strange ways, and why they had built their town so far from water.

Caleb enters with two empty buckets on a yoke, crosses and exits.

Settlers and Americans enter and mime the following as it is described.

Narrator 1 When Spring came we gave seed potatoes and tobacco seedlings to the Palefaces, but they gave us no thanks. Instead, they thanked their God.

Narrator 2 And when we showed them how to hunt bison, they begin to kill for sport and the herds diminished.

Narrator 1 But all our crops flourished, thanks to the Great Spirit.

Narrators It was a good year for tobacco and potato.

All go out. Enter Zaquo and Piquo each carrying a sack. They set them down with a sigh.

Piquo Last of the potato crop. I'm exhausted.

Zaquo I'll get Mina to carry them. (*Calling*) Mina!

Mina appears in the tent entrance.

Mina What now?

Zaquo Take these and boil some.

Mina Boiling is boring!

Zaquo Boiling is traditional!

Mina Well, Verity says …

Zaquo (*mocking*) 'Verity says'. From now on you keep away from those Paleface women! Chief's orders!

Mina But we promised to show them …

Zaquo Move!

Mina sighs, takes a sack and goes out.

Piquo	The less they have to do with the Palefaces, the better.
Zaquo	Yes. Yesterday she gave us something called Yorkshire pudding with our bison.
Piquo	What was it like?
Zaquo	It made me sick to look at it: I threw it to the dogs.
Piquo	And I'm getting sick of the Paleface men: they never heed our advice. What happened to that tobacco we gave them?
Zaquo	That reminds me: I've just cured some.
Piquo	Is it a cool smoke?
Zaquo	You'll never have a cooler smoke, I promise. Come and try it.

They enter the tent. Mina returns, picks up the other sack and peers inside the tent.

Mina Smoking's bad for you.

Zaquo appears with a long pipe.

Zaquo It'll be bad for you if you don't start on those potatoes! Move!

Piquo appears laughing, also with a pipe. Exit Mina.

Zaquo Is this a cool smoke or is it not?
Piquo Couldn't be cooler, man.

Caleb sings offstage.

Caleb My drink is water bright, water bright, water bright.
Zaquo Inside!

They go in the tent. Enter Caleb carrying the two buckets.

Caleb (*singing*) My drink is water bright, from the crystal stream.

He starts to cross the stage, stops, sniffs, then continues, singing.

Caleb	My drink is ... Smoke!

He sees smoke drifting from the tent.

And where there's smoke there's, er, there's, er ...

He puts down the yoke and picks up a bucket.

Fire!

He hurls the water into the tent. There are loud yells. He shouts 'Fire!' again and as Piquo appears, drenched, he throws the second bucketful over him, shouting 'Fire!' again. Piquo yells again.

Zaquo	(*appearing*) What are you doing? We were just starting to smoke!
Caleb	I was stopping you bursting into flames!
Piquo	You lily-faced loony! You were right about one thing, Zaquo.
Zaquo	What's that?
Piquo	You promised a cool smoke: that water's freezing!

Enter the Settler Men, Daffy, Hona and Zera.

Job	Where's the fire?
Piquo	There isn't one!
Job	So who shouted?
Caleb	Me. There was smoke coming from the tent, so I threw water in.
Zaquo	We were just smoking.
Amos	Just what?
Zaquo	You light tobacco in a pipe and inhale the smoke. All men do.

The Settlers back away, shuddering.

Settlers	Not us!
Pastor	The Bible does not speak of smoking!
Zaquo	And does the Bible speak of killing beasts for pleasure and leaving their carcasses to rot?

Zera Don't quarrel, you men! So what did you do with the tobacco leaves we gave you, Daffy?
Daffy We boiled them.

The Americans laugh.

Hona Boiled them! You didn't eat them, did you?
Daffy No: they tasted worse than weevils.
Zaquo You Palefaces never learn, do you?
Amos There's nothing you Indians can teach us, thank you!

There is a cheer offstage. Enter Verity.

Hona What's the cheering for?
Verity We've just cooked our first topatoes. We've looked forward to them for so long.
Hona How did you cook them?
Verity The way you said, I think.

Hope rushes in.

Verity What's wrong?
Hope Where's the salt?
Verity We'll show you.

Hope, Verity and Daffy hurry off.

Hona They seem to have got something right at last.

Mercy speaks from offstage.

Mercy Oh, no!
Hona What's that mean?
Zaquo It means they've got it wrong again. Here they come.

Enter the Settlers except Hope and Verity. The other Americans enter from the other side.

Job All you Indians have lied to us!
Settlers Yes!
Hona Why? What have we said?

The Burger Bar

Job You promised our women that topatoes were delicious!

Hona They are delicious!

Enter Verity with a deep dish and Hope with a bag.

Pastor (*pointing*) You call this disgusting mess delicious? I wouldn't feed pigs on this stuff! Look at it!

He lifts a dark green soggy mess from the dish.
Smell it!

Verity Topatoes! Huh!

The Americans point and fall about, howling and screaming with helpless laughter.

Zera speaks to Hondo.

Zera Why did you stop us women helping each other? They've boiled the leaves!

Verity Of course we've boiled the leaves!

Hope holds up potato roots with potatoes attached.

Hope What do you expect us to boil – these repulsive roots?

Settlers Yucch!

Verity What's wrong with them?

Piquo You tell us.

Hope They're all lumpy and deformed!

Settlers Deformed!

Verity Take these topatoes if you like them so much.

Americans Er …

Diva No thanks: we've just eaten.

Verity Anyone else?

Americans We've all just eaten.

Mercy We'd been so looking forward to the topato harvest: we're sick to the back teeth with boiled buffalo, aren't we?

Settlers Yes!

Rana	Have you tried turkey?
Pastor	Those ugly things! They're not mentioned in the Bible, like eagles and peacocks and doves. So who made them?
Settlers	The Devil!
Pastor	Yes, the Devil! Just like he made topatoes!
Amos	All those sackfuls of roots might spread disease!
Mina	(*entering*) We'll take them off your hands, won't we?

The American Women nod, trying not to laugh.

Faith	That's kind of you, Mina.
Mina	We all learn by our mistakes. Come on, we'll show you how to cook them.

All the Women start to go.

Hondo	Stop! Why are you going with the white women?
Aaron	And why are you mixing with the red women?
Faith	Because we talk more sense than you men! Come on, ladies!

All the Women hurry out, chattering and laughing. The two groups of Men glare at each other.

Hondo	Why don't you follow the squaws and learn cookery? You're not real men! You can't handle a bow; you don't even smoke!
Americans	No!
Aaron	We are true men who follow the way of the Lord!
Settlers	Amen!
Hondo	True men follow the Great Spirit!
Americans	Right!
Aaron	No! We've been here in India for a year now, and in all that time you've done nothing but hinder us!
Hondo	We've done nothing but try to help you!
Job	You want to gas us.
Zaquo	No, we want to teach you to smoke!

Isaac	You gave us topatoes to poison us!
Piquo	No, to feed you!
Pastor	And we've brought you the Christian message of love and peace!
Huso	Tell that to all the bison you've killed for sport!
Americans	Yeah!
Tonto	What can we eat when they've gone? The bison are our life.
Americans	Right!

Mina speaks from offstage.

Mina	Excuse me!

Mina enters wearing an apron, a chef's hat and a big smile. She sets up a billboard saying BURGERS COMING SOON.

Mina	Have a nice day!

She curtsies and exits. The Men stare.

Hondo	What's it say? I've forgotten my glasses.

Tonto reads the notice slowly.

Tonto	'Burgers coming soon.'
Caleb	Who's this Burger?
Job	Probably a messenger of God, like Isaiah or Jonah.

Daffy speaks offstage.

Daffy	Excuse me, gents!

Enter Daffy also wearing an apron and paper cap, carrying a litterbin which she puts down. It says KEEP AMERICA TIDY.

Caleb	Why are you working like that, Daffy?
Daffy	The squaws say if we all work together we could see a big profit.

She smiles, curtsies and exits.

Caleb	The big prophet Burger! I hope he brings news of peace for all men. I don't like quarrelling.

The Religious Leaders turn to address their followers.

Pastor	Friends, do not listen to this new prophet!
Medicine Man	Braves, close your ears to his cunning words!
Pastor	Because I tell you this!
Medicine Man	I say this!
Pastor	We have nothing in common with the Indians!
Settlers	No!
Medicine Man	The Paleface ways are not our ways!
Americans	No!
Pastor	They mock the message of Almighty God!
Medicine Man	They scorn the words of the Great Spirit!
Pastor	There is only one thing to do!
Medicine Man	One thing!
Pastor	We must fight them!
Settlers	Fight them!
Medicine Man	Fight!
Americans	Right!

Chanting 'Fight!' both sides grab weapons and line up facing each other. A war-drum beats and a bugle sounds. On each of the following lines one side steps back a pace, slowly raising their weapons. The Leaders raise their arms.

Hondo	Four!
Aaron	Three!
Hondo	Two!
Aaron	One!

The weapons are levelled facing each other and the drumming reaches a crescendo. Suddenly it stops and we hear a snatch of lively music, the Diner Song, (see below) as the Settler Women run on, all wearing aprons and caps, and grab their Men.

The Burger Bar

Settler Women Hold it! Hold it!
Settler Men What's happening?

The Squaws call offstage.

Squaws Hold it! Hold it!

The Squaws, also wearing aprons and caps, run on and hold their Men's arms.

Squaws Hold it!
American Men Hold what!
Women Hold everything!
Men Who do you think you are?
Women Who do we *think* we are? We *know* who we are!
Verity We are the women of America!
Aaron But a woman's place is in the house!
Piquo A squaw's place is in the tepee!
Aaron Weaving and sewing!
Piquo And pounding maize!
Women Not any more!
Isaac Will you women leave us men to fight in peace?

The Women let go of the Men and laugh.

Women 'To fight in peace'!
Mora How stupid can they get?
Isaac What I mean is …
Piquo What we mean is …
Isaac Today's the day for the showdown! Right, men?
Settler Men Right!
Hondo This is the day that decides the future! Right, braves?
American Men Right!
Verity Right, but not the way you men think! We women want to live together, not die together! Isn't that so?

The Women come forward.

Women That's so!

Zaquo How can we live together? We don't even eat the same food.

Zera From today we do! You men are stuck in your ways, but some of us women have been sharing recipes for months, even if they haven't all turned out right. There'll be no more boiled beef and bison at every meal!

Verity And no more salt pork! Come in, Mina!

Music. The Women yell and applaud as Mina enters pushing a mobile snackbar striped in white and red with a sign saying ALL-AMERICAN DINER. The Men clap as the Women open up the front to reveal a colourful interior. Singing, the Women hand menus to the Men, take their orders, hand out fast-food boxes and serve themselves.

Diner Song
(Tune: 'Bobby Shaftoe')

Women Here's the menu from our diner,
Better than the chow from China.

Daffy Beats the weevils on the liner!

Women Burgers from our diner!
Lick your lips and scan our menu,
Make your choice, look round and then you'll
See this is the coolest venue
In all Carolina!

Men Buns all packed with meat enticin',
Turkey burgers, fish or bison:
Try the Cheese and Veggie Nice 'Un
At our women's diner!

Mina Eat until your stomach's burstin'
Drink until there's no more thirstin',
Make sure next time you're the first in
Line at our diner!

Applause.

Mina	And to celebrate the grand opening of our All-American Women's Diner and Burger Bar, every customer receives a free portion of our brand-new speciality: American fries! Hand 'em out, girls!
Men	Wow! Fries!
	The Women serve everyone.
Women	Yes, American fries!
	Job tastes them.
Job	Well, folks, I'll say one thing about these American fries!
All	What's that?
Job	They taste a hundred times better than those darned topatoes!
Men	Hear, hear!
	Women laugh.
Pastor	Why are there no separate eating areas for reds and whites?
Faith	Because you told us to love our neighbours, Pastor, and these are our neighbours!
All	Hear, hear!
Medicine Man	Am I expected to eat a Cheese and Veggie Burger?
All	Yes!
	The Medicine Man tastes the burger.
Medicine Man	Yummy! It's even tastier than bison!
	All laugh.
Daffy	We ought to have an opening speech!
All	Hear, hear!
Pastor	May I say a few words …
All	No!
Aaron	Eat your fries, Pastor!
	All laugh.

Medicine Man	May I speak?
All	No!
Hondo	We men have said more than enough. Let the women have the final word!
Men	Hear, hear! Speech, Mina, Faith!

Mina holds up her hands for silence.

Mina	The message of this diner Is plain for all to see:
Faith	Don't look for where we differ, But where we most agree.
Mina	Let reds and whites together Come in from near and far
Both	To meet and eat and laugh and sing At the Women's Burger Bar!

All cheer.

The end

The Hole in the Wall

Bill Tordoff

List of Characters

Hadrian, *the Roman Emperor*
Pompous, *a Centurion*   Pompilia, *his wife*

Roman Soldiers	**British Women**	**Scotsmen**	**Hadrian's**
Dextrous, *a lance-corporal*	Liz	Alec	**Daughters**
	Flo	Angus	Amnesia
Amorous	Mog	Jock	Phobia
Devious	Peg	Mac	Trivia
Dubious	Sal	Wullie	Inertia
Laborious	Rose		Tibia
Studious			

Place: Hadrian's Wall

Time: Winter, AD 130

NOTES

The Wall: this can be represented by screens or a painted curtain or it can be constructed out of cardboard boxes or polystyrene blocks; alternatively it can be largely imaginary except for the minimum required for the opening ceremony.

Roman Numerals: The soldiers count as if the numerals were simply letters and not numbers: Eye, Vee, Ex, Ell, See, Dee, Em.

History: The Romans invaded England in AD 43 and gradually conquered most of Britain. The Emperor Hadrian crossed the Channel in about AD 122 and decided to build a wall from Wallsend-on-Tyne to Bowness-on-Solway to be the Northern frontier of the Empire, though he did not stay to see it built. Hadrian's Wall was finished in AD 130 and parts of it still stand today.

THE HOLE IN THE WALL

A freezing Winter's day on Hadrian's Wall. The wall is nearly finished except for a narrow gap. Four Roman soldiers, Amorous, Dextrous, Dubious and Laborious, are lowering a block of stone into position under the guidance of Pompous, a Centurion, who wears uniform including armour and a kilt. The Soldiers wear some uniform but have rough trousers under their kilts. There are a few benches or blocks.

Pompous	Hold that stone, men! Hold it! Hold it!
Amorous	We are holding it, sir! It's killing us!
Dextrous	Tell us what to do, sir, or we'll have to drop it!
Pompous	Left a bit. Left a bit. Left a bit. Right a bit. Down a bit. Gently! Steady! Right, let her go!

All groan, straighten up and inspect the Wall.

Dextrous	Eight years we've been building this wall.
Dubious	It's just about finished, isn't it, sir?
Pompous	Yes, thank Jupiter.

Laborious rubs his hands.

Laborious	Cor, Britain in Winter's like the Arctic!
Pompous	And it's even colder over there in Scotland.

Amorous speaks to Pompous.

Amorous	Why don't you wear trousers like us, sir? Keep your legs warm.
Pompous	Emperor's orders. My wife says …

Pompilia calls from offstage.

Pompilia	Pompous! Where are you?
Pompous	Over here, dear!

Pompilia	(*entering*) An officer's here with a message from Rome. Come and have a drink with him!
Pompous	Yes, dear. Er, carry on, men.

Pompous exits. The Soldiers try to hide their laughter. Pompilia glares at the Soldiers.

Pompilia	And don't you dare laugh at my husband! Why he lets you wear trousers I don't know! It's against orders!
Amorous	They keep us warm for our wives, missus.
Pompilia	Those British women are not your wives!
Laborious	They're as good as! Aren't they, lads?
Soldiers	Yes!
Pompilia	Roman soldiers are not allowed to marry foreign women, and you know it! If I were in charge I'd make you obey the rules. I'd have those trousers off for a start!
Soldiers	Cheeky!

Pompous calls from offstage.

Pompous	We're waiting, darling!

Pompilia glares at the Soldiers.

Pompilia	Oh! (*Calling*) Coming, darling!

Exit Pompilia.

Soldiers	(*mocking*) Coming, darling!
Dubious	What do we do now?
Laborious	Take it easy: I'm whacked! Where are the others?
Dextrous	Studious is still walking the wall. Devious is slacking, as usual.
Dubious	Here he comes.

Enter Devious through the gap. He looks round furtively.

Devious	Where's the officer?

Laborious	Never mind him! We're having to finish this wall without you. Where've you been?
Devious	At Jock's place. Those Scotties aren't half jumpy now the wall's nearly built.
Dubious	Why?
Devious	Jock reckons this gap's going to be walled up so nobody'll be able to get through.
Dextrous	Ah, he talks rubbish!
Laborious	He makes good whisky, though. Give us a swig.
Devious	Why should I?
Dextrous	'Cause it's freezing! And if you don't we'll tell the officer where you've been!
Devious	Oh, all right.

He produces a half bottle and hands it round.

Might be the last we ever have.

Studious speaks from offstage.

Studious	…MMMMMM, CM, LXXX, VIII.
Dubious	Here comes Studious at long last.

Studious enters pushing a solid surveyor's wheel, counting as he walks. (See notes.)

Studious … MMMMMM, CM, LXXX, IX. MMMMMM, CM, LXC. MMMM …

He looks up and realizes where he is.

Oh!

Dubious You've made it, Studious! Well done!

Studious stops and puts down the wheel. The Soldiers applaud.

Laborious You must be tired out! Have a whisky!

Studious tries to concentrate, takes out a small notebook and writes.

Wait! … MMMMMM, CM, LXIC! Right,

where's that drink?

He grabs the bottle and drinks deeply.

Devious Steady on!

Dextrous He deserves it: he's walked the whole length of the wall. How far is it?

Studious MMMMMM ...

Dextrous In figures!

Studious 76 Roman miles. And this is the only gap. It's very nearly finished.

Devious takes the bottle and looks at it.

Devious So is this!

Dubious Is it true we have to block the gap?

Studious You haven't heard half of it. After that we can ...

Rose enters through the gap.

Rose Studious! You're back!

Studious embraces her.

Studious Rosie!

Rose You smell of whisky!

Studious And you're cold.

He takes the bottle from Devious, who is on the point of drinking.

Here: get warm.

Rose Ooh, ta.

She drinks from the bottle.

Devious (*indignant*) Do you mind?

Rose No, I need it in this weather. I can't wait to go live in sunny Italy. Did you hear any news about it, pet?

Studious Yes. They say in Newcastle that all us builders'll be pensioned off now the wall's finished, then we can go back to Rome.

Soldiers	Hurray! Great!
Laborious	Back to Rome!
Dubious	A little farm for me!
Amorous	No more soldiering! No more stupid rules!

When This Lousy Wall Is Builded
(Tune: What a Friend We Have in Jesus)

Soldiers
When this lousy wall is builded
No more soldiering for me.
When I get my civvy clothes on
Oh how happy I shall be.

No more polishing my armour,
No more marching through the rain.
I'm going home to be a farmer.
And never leave Italy again.

Enter Flo, Liz, Mog, Peg and Sal through the gap.

Sal Here they all are.

She speaks to Rose.

Have you given him yours?

Rose Not yet.

Studious Given us what?

Liz Well, you've all worked so hard building this wall.

Women Hear, hear!

Mog And as it's nearly finished we've bought you all a present at the Scotty market.

The Women give small presents to their husbands.

Women Happy Wallday!
Well done!

Soldiers	Thank you very much!
Flo	What were you singing for?
Dubious	Shall we tell 'em?
Laborious	We'll have to.
Peg	Go on then.
Amorous	We can all leave the army, and we get either a pension or a free farm.
Flo	Where?
Amorous	Anywhere. But we're all going back to Italy, aren't we, lads?
Soldiers	Yes!
Women	(*happily*) Oh, Italy!
Rose	I've dreamed and dreamed of living in a warm country!
Women	Ooh, yes!
Studious	Wait a minute ...
Peg	No more cold feet!
Liz	Picking oranges and lemons off the trees!
Sal	Figs!
Flo	Olives!
Mog	Peaches!
Women	Magic!
Flo	When did you find out?
Rose	Just now. They told Studious in Newcastle.
Mog	It's wonderful!
Rose	When do we go, pet?
Studious	Erm, there's just one problem, Rosie.
Rose	What's that, pet?
Studious	Er, well, we shan't be able to take you women with us.
Women	What! Why not?

Dextrous	Because you're not Romans, so you're not properly married to us.
Women	Not properly married!
Flo	You must be joking!

Flo speaks to Amorous.

We've ground corn and baked and fetched water and washed your clothes and spun wool and woven cloth and cleaned your armour for ten pigging years! If that isn't marriage, what is?

Amorous	Don't blame us!
Mog	Who else can we blame?
Liz	When you first came we all had British boyfriends.
Women	Right!
Peg	But you bowled us over with your smart uniforms and your smooth talk.
Sal	And Italian food!
Rose	And wine! And cuddling us up on the back row of the theatre.
Women	Yes!
Flo	Our parents warned us! They said you Romans were all the same, but did we listen?
Women	No!
Rose	And the tales you told us!

Rose speaks to Studious.

You said you owned your own pizza parlour!

Liz speaks to Dextrous.

Liz	You told me we were going to open a pasta works in Bologna!
Sal	And you all swore you had your own chariots back in Italy!
Women	Right!

Mog speaks to Devious.

Mog You were the worst! All those lies about picking the spaghetti harvest off the bushes!

The Soldiers laugh.

Peg It's not funny! We've lived with you for ten years 'cause you said you'd marry us as soon as you could and take us back to Italy.

Liz And now you're ditching us!

Dextrous We'll write to you.

Liz Big deal!

Dextrous You'll find British husbands.

Liz Where? Most of 'em are in the army in Africa.

Sal Anyway, you've spoiled us for them: you've shown us a better way of life.

Dubious You'll be all right on your own.

Peg How? Once this camp's closed there won't be any jobs.

Rose And once that gap's closed we can't shop in the Scotty market, either.

Liz Don't you like me, Dextrous?

Dextrous 'Course I like you! And I wish I could marry you properly, then we could live in Bologna, but we can't. It's the rule.

Liz Who made this rule?

Dextrous The Emperor, I suppose.

Mog Why?

Devious We don't know!

Studious I suppose you want your gifts back?

Rose No, keep 'em! It's you we want.

Peg Right! We're not giving you up, are we, girls?

Women No way!

A trumpet sounds a brief call.

Dextrous	Back to work. The officer's coming.
Flo	Let's go talk this over while we cook the dinner, girls.
Mog	Right: hurry!

The Women hurry out. Enter Pompous frowning and carrying a scroll. The Soldiers line up raggedly, pocketing their presents.

Dextrous	All presents, er, present and correct, sir!
Pompous	Stand easy, men.
Amorous	You look cold, sir.
Devious	And worried.
Pompous	Yes. A message has just arrived from Rome.
Dubious	Can we go home, sir?
Pompous	Not yet, I'm afraid.
Soldiers	Aw!
Devious	Why not, sir?
Pompous	Because we have to close up that gap first.
Laborious	The women won't like that, sir.
Pompous	Those women don't matter!
Studious	Try telling them that!
Dextrous	Silence in the ranks!
Pompous	The big news is that the Emperor Hadrian himself will soon be here to open the wall!
Soldiers	The Emperor himself?
Pompous	Yes, and he's in a foul mood. He's had a bad cold ever since he landed so don't upset him or he might keep us here.
Soldiers	Oh, no!

Laborious raises his hand.

Laborious	Sir, I've been thinking. Why should we close the wall if the Emperor's going to open it again?
Soldiers	Hear, hear!

Pompous	Are you stupid? When I say open it, I don't mean open it.

The Soldiers look disgusted.

Soldiers	Aw!
Dextrous	Quiet! When the officer says open it, he doesn't mean open it! What *do* you mean, sir?
Pompous	I mean he will officially name it Hadrian's Wall, and knock the last nail into a plaque saying that he built it.
Laborious	But he didn't build it, sir: we did!
Soldiers	Hear, hear!
Pompous	You built it in his name! He planned it! He put in the brainwork!

Laborious raises his hand again.

Laborious	Sir, the inscription could say he put in the brainwork and we put in the real work.
Pompous	We've no time to waste! Wall up the gap, now! Studious, carve the inscription.
Dextrous	Sir, there's no time to wall it up properly!
Pompous	Well, fill it in the best way you can!
Dextrous	Yes, sir! Attention! Right turn! By the left, quick march!

The Soldiers march off, passing Pompilia who enters in haste.

Pompilia	Pompous! He'll be here any minute!
Pompous	Who?
Pompilia	The Emperor himself! And he's bringing his daughters: Amnesia, Phobia, Trivia, Tibia and Inertia!

Pompous laughs.

Pompilia	Stop laughing: they can't help their names!
Pompous	They must be mad, coming to Britain in midwinter!

Pompilia	The rumour is that they're desperate to find husbands. They say Roman men are too soft.
Pompous	Well, they're wasting their time up here.

Dextrous speaks from offstage.

Dextrous	Left, right! Left, right! Left, right!

Dextrous enters followed by Laborious, Dubious and Amorous carrying a screen and Studious carrying a slab.

Dextrous	Halt, one two! Screen party and scribe, sir!
Pompous	Hurry! The Emperor will soon be here!
Dextrous	Yes, sir! By the left …
Pompilia	Wait!
Dextrous	Hold it!
Pompilia	Pompous, these soldiers are indecently and incorrectly dressed. Wearing trousers like Eastern women! What will the Emperor say?
Dextrous	Sir! If we're going to finish the job in this weather we need warm clothes.
Pompilia	No, it's against the rules, Pompous!
Soldiers	Sir …!
Pompous	Quiet! You may wear trousers as long as you're working in the cold. But if you see the Emperor …
Pompilia	Or his daughters: Amnesia, Phobia, Trivia, Tibia and Inertia …

The Soldiers laugh.

Pompous	Stop laughing: they can't help their names!

The Soldiers stand stifling their laughter.

Pompous	If you see them you must roll your trousers up. Understood?

The Soldiers nod.

Pompous	Good. Carry on!

Soldiers Sir!

During the following the Soldiers use the screen to mask the gap and disappear behind it. We hear occasional hammering.

Pompilia I must go and change! Such a thrill to meet the Emperor! What gifts have you bought him, dear?

Pompous Oh, just a few trifles.

Pompilia Trifles? Leave the food to me!

Pompous I mean small gifts: fifty silver shields, a hundred gold-plated spears, a statue of Jupiter. That sort of trifle.

Pompilia But his daughters will want gifts, too! We can't give them spears.

Pompous By Jove, you're right! What can we get for them?

Devious enters furtively carrying an empty sack and disappears behind the screen.

Pompilia You! Soldier!

Devious reappears.

Devious Me, madam?

Pompilia Yes, where are you going with that sack?

Devious I was just popping across to the Scotty market before the gap's closed, madam.

Pompilia Trading with the enemy! Flog him and drag him behind a chariot, Pompous!

Devious (*kneeling*) No! Spare me, sir! Please!

Pompous Quiet! So you were going to the Scots market, eh?

Devious I won't go, sir! I swear it!

Pompous Yes, you will!

Devious No, I won't! I mean, I will if you say so, sir!

Pompous takes out a purse.

Pompous Here's a purseful of gold to buy gifts for the Emperor's five daughters.

Devious	Gifts for daughters. Yes, sir.

There is a burst of hammering from behind the screen.

Pompous	And hurry back before that gap's closed!
Devious	Trust me, sir!

Devious hurries out behind the screen.

Pompilia	Trust him? You won't see that gold again.
Pompous	He's our only hope. Let's get ready.

They go out. There is a burst of coughing from behind the screen and all the Soldiers except Devious stagger out.

Studious	We should have masks against that dust!
Laborious	Yes, it's a danger to health.
Dextrous	Army life *is* dangerous! Get back behind that screen, all of you!
Soldiers	No!

Enter Amnesia, Phobia, Trivia, Inertia and Tibia, unseen by the quarrelling soldiers. They smile when they see the soldiers, and stand rubbing their hands.

Dextrous	I'm giving you ten to get back to work! I! II! III! IV! V! VI! VII! VIII! IX!
Daughters	(*laughing*) X!
Soldiers	(*turning*) Oh, no!

They look down at their trousers in embarrassment.

Dextrous	Men! Trousers: roll up! Sorry, ladies, we didn't see you.

The Soldiers try to roll their trousers up while the Daughters laugh and whistle.

Phobia	Pull 'em up!
Amnesia	Show us a leg!
Daughters	Yes!
Dextrous	I'm afraid they won't stay up.

Daughters	Oh, shame!
Inertia	Take 'em off, then!
Daughters	Yes! Get 'em off!
Laborious	But if we take them off we're too cold to work.
Dubious	And we have to finish the wall because the Emperor himself is coming with his five ... Oh, you're his daughters!
Daughters	Correct!
Amnesia	Amnesia!
Phobia	Phobia!
Trivia	Trivia!
Tibia	Tibia!
Inertia	And Inertia!

The Soldiers try not to laugh.

Dextrous	Pleased to meet you! Back behind the screen, men!
Trivia	Stop! Let's have a look at you!
Studious	But we must finish the wall!
Tibia	Never mind that! Turn round and show us your legs!

Embarrassed, the Soldiers obey. The Daughters confer.

Amnesia	What do you think, girls?
Phobia	They're only common soldiers, aren't they?
Daughters	(*depressed*) Yes.
Inertia	And their legs aren't all that good, are they?
Daughters	(*depressed*) No.
Trivia	But this is the furthest point of the Empire. There are no more men in the world.
Inertia	Except hairy barbarians like Eskimos and Scots.
Tibia	And who's going to live on haggis and whalemeat?
Phobia	What a life! Half the men we meet laugh at our names and the other half don't have what we're seeking.

Trivia	And what are we seeking?
Tibia	Smart husbands with splendid legs!

They face the audience and hum.

Legs

Trivia	There are some things magic in a man that every girl in the civilized world agrees on.
Tibia	But other things turn different people on and off for no apparent reason.
Amnesia	Like, some girls when they see a man will say 'What wicked eyes!'
Phobia	But some like best a massive chest of Schwarzenegger size.
Inertia	Some swoon at more artistic types with pale and soulful faces, Who murmur gentle poetry in passionate embraces.
Trivia	But for me there are only two things about a man that really matter!
Tibia	I don't care if his face looks as if it's just been run over in a chariot race so that it's as flat as a Roman pancake or even flatter!
Trivia	Fact, most of male anatomy Is lacking in éclat to me 'Cause all I care about is legs. Ooh!

Song

All	We just dream about legs! Ooh! A pair of thighs and a couple of calves: We girls don't do things by halves! We want two! We want two! Ooh, ooh, ooh, ooh, ooh!
Inertia	Men in trousers fail to arouse us.

Trivia	They don't make us squeal!
Tibia	Tartan trews are plain bad news: They simply don't reveal!
Inertia	But at a tunic or a kilt Our resistance starts to wilt,
Amnesia	And we know we didn't oughter,
Phobia	But we wish that they were shorter, So we could see more legs!
All	Legs, legs, legs! Legs, legs, legs! Ooh, ooh, ooh, ooh, ooh! (*wistfully*) Oooh!

The Soldiers clap half-heartedly.

Soldiers Very nice.

They start to move off behind the screen.

Trivia Wait!
Soldiers (*stopping*) Aw, no!
Trivia What do you say, girls? Shall we have 'em or not?
Daughters (*shrugging*) Why not?
Trivia Right!

Trivia speaks to Amorous.

You!
Amorous Who, me?
Trivia Yes, come here! What's your name?
Amorous Amorous.
Trivia I love the sound of that! Are you married, Amorous?
Amorous Er, not legally. None of us are.
Trivia Well, you're in luck. What would you say if I told you I wanted to marry you?

Flo appears in an apron carrying a pan and a spoon.

Flo I'd say you must be mad, lady!

Phobia	Don't call my sister mad!
Flo	Why not?
Phobia	'Cause it makes her mad!
Flo	Well, she must be, wanting my man! He's only a common soldier: they all are.
Amnesia	They won't be common when they're married to us! Grab 'em, girls!

The Daughters squabble over the Soldiers and end up each grabbing one by the arm while Flo beats the pan like a gong. Enter the other Women.

Liz	What's going on?
Flo	These spoiled Italian layabouts are stealing our men!
Inertia	We're not spoiled and they're not yours!

The Women cross to their Men and grab their other arms.

Women	Oh yes, they are!
Daughters	Oh no, they're not!
Mog	Ask them! What do you say, lads? Who do you want to go with?

The Soldiers look from one woman to another.

Soldiers	Erm, er …

A fanfare starts to sound.

Dextrous	The Emperor! Quick, men!

The Soldiers hurry behind the screen as Pompous hurries on wearing his ceremonial uniform.

Pompous	Line up, everyone! Make way for the Emperor!

The Women stand on one side, the Daughters on the other.

Pompous	Where's the guard of honour?

Dextrous speaks from offstage.

Dextrous	Behind here, sir!
Pompous	Remove that screen at once!

Dextrous speaks from offstage.

Dextrous	We can't, sir: we're changing!

Pompous speaks to the Daughters.

Pompous	I wonder if you ladies could, er …
Daughters	You must be joking!
Peg	Show 'em, girls!

The Women remove the screen, revealing the gap filled with a stone-painted flat which includes the official plaque saying HADRIANUS HOC MURUM FECIT CXXX AD, and the Soldiers who have removed their trousers and are changing into their uniforms. The Daughters scream with laughter. The Women grab the trousers and stand back. Enter Hadrian with Pompilia on his arm. The Women applaud and the Soldiers line up. (During the following, the Women put on the trousers.)

Dextrous	Honour guard, attention! Present arms!

Hadrian sneezes.

All	Bless you!
Pompous	Ladies, soldiers, female British peasants …
Women	Charming!
Pompous	Quiet! It gives me very great …

Hadrian sneezes.

All	Bless you!
Pompous	Very great pleasure to welcome the Emperor Hadrian.

All applaud.

Hadrian	Well, it doesn't give *me* pleasure! I'm freezing to death and I have a wicked cold, so let's get it over with!

Trivia	Father, you've forgotten something!
Hadrian	What?
Daughters	Our presents!
Hadrian	Where are my daughters' presents, Pompilia?
Pompilia	They'll be here quite soon, your Majesty.

Hadrian sneezes.

All	Bless you!
Hadrian	Shut up! 'Quite soon'? They always get what they ask for immediately! What do you want, girlies?
Daughters	Those soldiers!
Women	(*despairing*) Oh, no!
Pompilia	We'll deliver them gift-wrapped straight after the ceremony, your Majesty!
Hadrian	That's better!

He surveys the stopgap.

This wall isn't even finished!

Pompous	Straight after the ceremony, your Majesty!
Hadrian	Well, what do I do?
Pompilia	You make a little speech and knock in the final nail, then we sing a couple of songs.

Fanfare.

Pompous	The Emperor Hadrian will now declare his wall open!

All applaud as Hadrian mounts a block next to the plaque.

Hadrian	I have built this wall to keep in everything that is Roman and polished and civilized, and to keep out everything barbaric and rough and hairy, especially Scots and Eskimos.
All	Hear, hear!
Hadrian	I name it Hadrian's Wall and take pleasure in knocking in this gold nail.

He sneezes. Studious hands him a silver hammer and holds a large gold nail in the edge of the plaque. He hits the nail twice and pauses to blow his nose. The stopgap shudders as it is hit twice from the other side. All stare. He hits it again three times. It is hit again three times from the other side.

Hadrian What's happening?

A strange wailing fills the air.

Hadrian What is it?
Pompilia It's ghosts!
Daughters Ghosts! Aargh!

The wailing turns into a tune on the bagpipes.

Pompous It's the Scots! Death or glory! To arms, men!
Dextrous To arms!

The Soldiers draw their weapons. The Daughters scream again as the stopgap falls with a bang. Through the gap march the Scots led by a piper playing 'Scotland the Brave'. They are in full splendour including two swords per man, kilts, sporrans and stockings with skean-dhus. They march round the stage and line up. The music ends.

Alec Draw your swords!
Dextrous On guard, Romans!

The Soldiers level their weapons and the Others exclaim and recoil as the Scots draw their swords, only to lay them down. The bagpipes sound again and the Scots perform a sword-dance, lifting their kilts as they finish. The Daughters clap madly.

Hadrian Who are you and what are you doing here?
Alec Tell the gentleman who we are, lads!
Scots We're the Braw Lads of Kinlochstrachan, the noo!
All The what, the noo?

Alec	The Braw Lads of Kinlochstrachan. You ken, each year the lassies of Kinlochstrachan pick oot …
All	Pick oot?
Alec	Aye! They pick oot the lads with the finest legs to walk the bounds of the parish and dance at every corner. Am I right?
Scots	You're right, Alec!
Angus	Now someone has gone and built this great thing right across the corner!
Mac	And they're even talking of filling in the gap!
Jock	Aye, we'd like to meet the chap who planned this wall! We'd tell him a thing or two!
Scots	Aye, that we would!
Hadrian	And what would you say to me if I told you that *I* planned it?
	Wullie shakes his hand.
Wullie	We'd just say it'll make a first-class tourist attraction, sir!
Scots	Hear, hear!
Hadrian	Well, thank you!
Angus	Nice meeting you, sir, but we must push on.
Jock	Aye, it could snow.
Alec	Let's march awa', lads!
Daughters	Stop!
Scots	What?
Daughters	Don't go!
Trivia	You've got the finest legs we've ever seen! Marry us!
Scots	Marry you?
Inertia	Yes! And come with us back to Rome, where the sun shines all the year!
Phobia	We'll buy you all silk-lined kilts!
Amnesia	And golden swords!

Tibia	And you can perform in the Colosseum twice a day, and three times on Saturn's day!
Phobia	What do you say? Please!

The Scots look at each other and nod.

Scots	All right!

Hadrian sneezes.

All	Bless you!
Trivia	Give us these tartan-wrapped hunks, father!
Tibia	Then we'll be off your hands for good.
Daughters	Please, Daddy!

Hadrian blows his nose.

Hadrian	You said you wanted these others.
Pompilia	Your Majesty! By law, Romans are not allowed to marry barbarians!
Amnesia	They're not barbarians: they're the smartest men we've ever seen!
Pompous	And think of your own feelings!
Hadrian	I *am* thinking of my own feelings! I'm freezing, and I've a stinking cold that no one cares about and nothing can cure!

He sneezes. Jock holds up a hand.

Jock	Whisht, man! Dinna say that! Try a wee dram of this!

He produces a bottle from his sporran and gives it to Hadrian. Hadrian sniffs it.

Hadrian	What is it?
Jock	The water of life. Triple-distilled whisky.
All	Triple-distilled!
Jock	Aye. It's guaranteed to bring the dead to life within an hour, or cure a common cold in ten seconds flat.
Hadrian	Ten seconds?

Jock	I promise you.
Hadrian	If it doesn't cure me in ten seconds I'll have you executed on the spot as a warning to all liars, and if it does you can all marry my girls.

He sneezes and drinks.

All	I! II! III! IV! V! VI! VII! VIII! IX! X!

Hadrian takes a deep breath and smiles.

Hadrian	I'm cured! It's magic!
All	Hurray!
Hadrian	Come back to Rome and marry my girls and we'll all drink whisky at the wedding!
Pompilia	But, your Majesty, the law says that Romans cannot marry …!
Hadrian	I am the law! And I say that from now Romans can marry whoever they choose!

The Daughters each grab a Scot.

Daughters	And we choose you!

The Women grab their men.

Women	And we're married to you! Hurray!
All	Hurray!

Trivia speaks to Jock.

Trivia	And we can open the first distillery in Rome!

Liz speaks to Dextrous.

Liz	And we'll have the first spaghetti factory in Bologna!
Dextrous	Spaghetti Bolognese! I like the sound of it!

Devious calls from offstage.

Devious	Wait! Wait!

All stare as Devious appears in the gap, drops his sack and stands panting.

Hadrian	Who's this?
Pompous	Another of my men, sir.

Pompous speaks to Devious.

Where are the surprise gifts for the Emperor's daughters?

Devious points to the sack.

Devious	In there, sir.
Trivia	Surprise gifts! Come on, girls!

Screaming, the Daughters snatch the sack and disappear through the gap.

Pompous The next item is a little song from your loyal troops, sir. Forward, men!

Applause as all the Soldiers and Pompous line up.

We Wouldn't Give Twopence for England
(Tune: My Bonnie Lies Over the Ocean)

Soldiers
We wouldn't give twopence for England,
'Cause twopence is more than it's worth.
It's foggy, it's damp and it's freezing:
The dreariest spot upon earth!

Our homeland is over the Channel,
Our homeland is over the sea.
There's good food and good wine and sunshine,
And that is where we want to be.

Applause. The Soldiers gesture towards the gap. Enter the Daughters wearing tartan tams and scarves. The Piper plays as the Soldiers replace the stopgap, then the Daughters pair off with the Scots and the Women with the Soldiers.

Hadrian	Is everyone ready now to march to Italy?
All	We are!
Hadrian	And do you have a marching song?

All We do!

Hadrian Then sing as we go!

> ***The Squaddies are Marching Home***
> *(Tune: When Johnny comes Marching Home)*

All (*singing and marching*)

> The Squaddies are marching home again. Hurrah! Hurrah!
> We're marching back to Rome again. Hurrah! Hurrah!
>   Oh, we're the lads who built the wall
>   They said could never be built at all,
> But there it stands as the Squaddies come marching home.
>
> The Squaddies are marching home again. Hurrah! Hurrah!
> We're marching back to Rome again. Hurrah! Hurrah!
>   The folk will cheer, the boys will shout,
>   The cats and dogs will all turn out
> And we'll dance all night when the Squaddies come marching home.

The end

Kaa!

Bill Tordoff

Music by Paul Woodhouse

List of Characters

The Gas family	**Tree Kids**	**Oil Workers**
(*from America*)	Sib, *their blind leader*	Amis
Boss Gas, *an oilman*	Meg	Ford
Citronella, *his wife*	Fly	Park
Chunky ⎱ *their sons*	Eva	Tate
Beefy ⎰	Jem	Beck
Honey ⎱ *their daughters*	Rio	Nash
Candy ⎰	Jon	Snow
	Ann	West
	Mac	
	Sam	

Place: A forest clearing in a remote semi-tropical country.

Time: The present.

NOTES
1. **The Car** can be as elaborate or as simple as your resources allow. It can even be represented by offstage sound effects.
2. **The Orchid** – the head can be moved from behind like a glove puppet or remotely controlled by a fishing line.
3. **The Posters** should be big enough to dominate the stage.
4. **Lines allocated to 'All', 'Girls' etc**. will not always be spoken by all the group. Exactly who speaks can be agreed in rehearsal.
5. **Songs** appear on page 88 – 'It's a Gas', page 91 – 'We're gonna be Rich'; page 100 – 'Gasco Gang Song', page 101 – 'Hexacola', and page 106 – 'Kaa Worship'. The music for these songs can be found at the end of the book on pages 107–111.

KAA!

A clearing in a semi-tropical forest. Birdsong can be heard. A cooking pot is on a fireplace, with a water pot. There is a mug-tree with enough mugs for the Tree Kids. Downstage at one side is the Magic Orchid, a large, many-leaved plant with a large bud on its single stalk. Suddenly a small animal screams in fright, offstage.

From offstage.

Mac There's one!

Fly After it! Kill it!

Fly, a barefoot boy wearing dirty shorts, carrying a catapult and a game bag, runs on, fires and angrily cries 'Missed!' Enter Mac, similarly dressed. They stop, out of breath.

Fly Dang, dang, dang! Only one we've seen all day! What's going wrong, Mac?

Mac Dunno: forest used to be full of game. It's going to be a miserable New Year feast tonight.

Fly looks in the water pot.

Fly There's no water either. Where are all the girls? (*Calling*) Sib! Eva! Meg!

Mac Someone's here.

Jon, Sam and Jem run in, dressed like the others.

Mac Caught anything?

Jem Only a little one.

Jon produces a cylinder about 30cm long.

Jon Hey, we found this, though.

Mac examines the cylinder.

Mac	It says 'Gasco. 30-second fuse' and ...

Mac gives the cylinder to Fly.

Here.

Fly reads the label with difficulty.

Fly	'Sem. Tex. Explo ...' Can't read it.
Sam	Hey, there could be food inside!

Mac picks up a rock.

Mac	Yes! Hit it where it says 'Detonator'!
Fly	What's that mean?
Sam	Dunno: just bash it!
Fly	All right.

He puts down the cylinder and takes the rock.

Fly	Here goes!

There is an echoing boom from offstage and the cries of birds. They stare.

Mac	That was nearer.
Jem	Here come the girls: they look worn out.

Enter the Girls except Sib, carrying water containers, which are mainly empty. They wear rough dresses and are barefoot.

Eva	Have you caught anything for the feast?

Jem holds up a tiny furry animal.

Jem	Yes, this.

The girls drop the containers and look depressed.

Girls	Aw!
Meg	That's all we need!
Jon	What else is wrong?
Meg	The well's drying up.
Boys	Oh, no!

Girls	Oh, yes!
Sam	But I'm thirsty!
	Eva offers her container to Sam.
Eva	Here, mighty hunter!
Sam	Oh, thanks:
	Sam drinks some water and spits it out.
	Yaargh! It's disgusting!
	All laugh.
Rio	It's not funny: that's all there is.
Jem	Well, you'll have to get it from the river.
Rio	We're not spending our lives walking that far, are we?
Girls	No way!
Sam	Well, *we're* not!
Boys	No!
Meg	So what do we do? We can't live without water.
Rio	We'll have to move near the river.
Eva	We can't: she left this forest to us. Anyway, the orchid's here and it yields at midnight.
	All look at the orchid, close their eyes and breathe in deeply. Music.
Ann	No orchid means no youth and no life.
Jon	No water means no life.
	Meg breaks the mood.
Meg	We're not going to have much life at the feast tonight: one bushbaby, stale breadfruit and dirty water!
	There is another echoing explosion, nearer. All stare.
Ann	It's getting nearer. What can it be?
Fly	Ask Sib: she's here.
	Sib appears, a tall, blind girl carrying a carved staff. Round her neck is a silver phial on a thong. She crosses to the orchid.

Ann   What makes that noise, Sib? Is it gods shaking the earth?

Sib sniffs the orchid.

Sib   It's outsiders, frightening the beasts and drying up the well.

Jem   Outsiders can't come! This land's ours!

All listen. Faintly, we hear a car, then the Gas family singing.

Eva   They're here! Hide!

All hide. Fly runs back to snatch the cylinder. A musical car horn sounds, then into the clearing crashes a car (see note) containing the Gas family. Boss wears a moustache, a bush jacket and khaki trousers, a baseball cap and a revolver. Citronella, his wife, wears a black dress and high-heels. She has long hair and is heavily made up, with long red nails. Chunky and Beefy, their sons, wear baseball caps and tracksuits with Gasco logos and smaller badges. Honey and Candy, their daughters, wear pastel shellsuits. They and their mother wear SAVE THE TREES badges. All hold cola cans or junk food. They are singing:

Song: It's a Gas

Gases   Cruisin' 'long o' Main Street: it's a gas!
Burnin' up the thruway: it's a gas!
Drivin' thru' the forest: it's a gas!
   Anytime, any place: it's a gas!

Watchin' drive-in movies: it's a gas!
Rootin' at the ball-game: it's a gas!
Hootin', tootin', scootin': it's a gas!
   Anytime, any place: it's a gas!

French fries, popcorn: it's a gas!
Doughnuts, burgers: it's a gas!
Cola, soda: it's a gas!
   Fast cars, fast food: life's a gas!

Citronella	Stop, stop, stop!
Boss	(*stopping*) What is it, darling?
Citronella	(*inhaling*) A magic perfume filling the forest air!
Boss	My perfume's petroleum! Unless we find some soon, Gasco's finished. Hard-hats on, kids! Who's going to explode the last charge?

Boss produces a cylinder like the one the Tree Kids found.

All put on hard-hats.

Beefy	Me, Paw!
Chunky	No, he lost one yesterday, Paw!
Citronella	Quiet!

She sprays herself, then the air, with perfume.

The Gas family do not disturb the environment. Do we, my pets?

Girls	Gee, no, Maw: we're environmentally friendly!
Beefy	You're environmentally stupid.
Boss	Shut up! This is our final chance to strike it rich.

He gives Chunky the cylinder.

Chunky, walk over there, stick this in the ground and hurry back afore she blows.

Chunky	Aw, Paw, walkin' ain't natural!

Citronella produces a brightly coloured packet of biscuits.

Citronella	This giant pack of Hexie cookies says you can do it, sweetheart!

Chunky takes the packet.

Chunky	I'd do anything for Hexies!

Exit Chunky with the cylinder and the packet.

Gas Kids	We want Hexies too, Maw!
Citronella	All watch the seismograph. Here.

She gives Candy a seismograph.

Boss And all pray we find oil.

Chunky speaks from offstage.

Chunky Twenty-second fuse starting now!
All One, two, three, four, five, six ...

Candy continues to count.

Citronella Hurry back, darling, before she blows!
Candy Eleven, twelve, thirteen ...

She shakes the seismograph.

Come on! We want to hear you bleep!

Citronella shouts at Candy.

Citronella Stop that!

Chunky speaks from offstage.

Chunky I've stopped, Maw!
Citronella Not you, darling: run!
Boss She's going to blow! Hit the deck, son!
Candy Nineteen, twenty!

All crouch down, fingers in their ears. There is a loud explosion offstage. Chunky yells and a shower of leaves falls. The seismograph bleeps loudly.

Honey The bleeper's hit a hundred!
All A hundred! Wow!

Chunky sobs loudly offstage, then staggers in, weeping. His face is blackened. The other Gas Kids laugh.

Citronella He can hardly walk! Come to Mommy, baby.

She wipes Chunky clean.

Boss I guess he'll never walk again.
Citronella He'll never walk? You don't mean ...?

Boss	I mean we're going to be so rich that these kids'll be driving their own cars!
Kids	Our own cars? Zowee!
Boss	Yes! This seismograph says there's a giant sea of oil under this forest!
All	Yahoo!
Boss	Gasco's going to erect drilling rigs here, and a refinery and gas stations and black tarmac thruways that'll make us mega-rich! Tell the world!

Song: We're gonna be Rich

All	We're gonna be rich, rich, rich! We're gonna be rich, rich, rich! We're gonna be stinking, stinking, stinking rich!
Boys	I'm going to have a car that I can call my own!
Girls	And we will have two others for ourselves alone
Candy	With a great big built-in microwave
Honey	And gold-plated phone!
All	We're gonna be rich, rich, rich!
Citronella	I'm going to have a bedroom just as wide as the sky And the closet for my outfits will be ten storeys high: I'll buy a million pairs of shoes and if you ask me why:
All	She's gonna to be rich, rich, rich!
Boss	We'll drink so much that there will be a bottling boom
Honey	They'll have to pull down Everest to make sure there's room
Candy	For all those mountains of food that we are going to consume!

All	We're gonna to be rich, rich, rich! Hurray!
Boss	We have to find who owns this land and screw the drilling rights out of 'em, fast!
Beefy	Aw, what's the hurry?
Boss	The hurry is our licence expires at midnight, dumbo!
Honey	Looks like someone lives here: there's a fireplace and some slimy stuff in this cook thing.

Honey and Candy look in the pot.

Honey and Candy	Yuccch!
Boss	All shout!
All	(*calling*) Anybody home?

Citronella sniffs the perfume of the orchid.

Citronella	You beauty! You smell of youth's young dream!
Candy	I spy! Come out, whoever you are!

Sam shyly emerges. The Gases clap.

Boss	A native kid! Sweet-talk him, Candy. Ask who owns the land.
Candy	(*smiling*) You live round here, boy?

Sam nods.

Candy	You got a Maw and Paw?

Sam shakes his head.

Candy	You got a family?

Sam nods.

Candy	And do they own this land?

Sam nods.

Boss	That's fantastic! Anybody else hiding?

All the hidden Tree Kids say 'Me!' in succession.

Citronella	They're all around! Come out!

All the Tree Kids appear while the Gases laugh and clap.

Boss Let's say a big 'Hi' to all our forest friends!

The Gases all smile and speak loudly.

Gases Hi there, forest friends!

The Tree Kids smile shyly but stay silent.

Citronella They've lost their tongues!
Honey It's not all they're going to lose!

The Gases laugh.

Citronella Quiet, sweety.
Boss Who's going to speak? Anybody.

There is silence.

Come on, open up! What do you have to say?

Sib steps forward.

Sib Why are you here?
Boss (*applauding*) Good question! And the answer is – we've come to help.
Sib We don't need anything!

She speaks to the Kids.

Do we?

Kids No!
Ann Well, except …
Citronella Hold it!

She crosses to Ann.

What's your name, beautiful?

Ann Ann.
Citronella I think you people do need something, don't you, Ann?

Ann nods.

Citronella	Is it something very valuable?

Ann nods.

Citronella	What is it?
Ann	Water. Our well's dried up.

Chunky and Beefy laugh scornfully.

Chunky and Beefy	Water, valuable?
Boss	No problem! Boys: bring river water and lots of it, now!
Rio	It takes a whole day!
Chunky	No way! Let's go, brother!
Beefy	One of you kids like a car ride?
Jem	Me!
Chunky and Beefy	Hop aboard, bunny!

Chunky, Beefy and Jem roar off in the car with the radio playing. The Tree Kids all stare as it disappears.

Tree Kids	Wow!
Boss	Introduction time! We're the Gas family from Texas. Those are our sons, Beefy and Chunky, and these are our beautiful daughters.
Candy	Hello, I'm Candy.
Honey	Hi, I'm Honey.
Citronella	My name's Citronella. You can call me Mommy.
Boss	And you can call me Boss! Hi there!
Tree Kids	Hi, there, Boss!
Citronella	Do you children live on your own?

Tree Kids nod.

Candy	You get your own food and all?

Tree Kids nod.

Honey	And you don't go to school?

Tree Kids shake their heads.

Boss	So how long have you been here?

Fly	Since Mrs Norris brought us.
Citronella	That's impossible!
Boss	What's wrong? Who's Mrs Norris?

We hear the car-horn and engine and Chunky, Jem and Beefy appear with plastic water containers.

Beefy and Chunky	Water, water, water!
Tree Kids	Wow! Wonderful! Here in no time!
Chunky	Come and get it!

As the smiling Gas Kids give water to the Tree Kids, Boss takes Citronella aside.

Jem	Hey, that car thing's magic!
Sib	(*sniffing*) It smells foul.
Boss	These youngsters are eating out of our hand!
Citronella	They are not youngsters!
Boss	What do you mean?
Citronella	They say Mrs Norris brought them! But she disappeared with a boatload of babies in 1945!
Boss	So?

Citronella points to the Tree Kids.

Citronella	So they are fifty years old! What's their secret?
Boss	Forget that now: we need those drilling rights!

He smiles and speaks to the Tree Kids.

So, who's the big boss on this island?

Tree Kids	Our God.
Boss	Your God, hey?

He winks at his family.

So where's he live?

Fly	Everywhere. He's inside us.
Boss	Is that so?

He winks again.

Then you can answer for him, hey?

Fly	Answer who?

Chunky points at the name on his tracksuit.

Chunky	Us: Gasco!
Beefy	The Gas Family Exploitation Company!
Boss	That bang just now tells us there could be a little oil here. You know oil?
Ann	The orchid gives oil at midnight every New …
Kids	Ann! Shh!

Citronella speaks as if thinking aloud.

Citronella	Does it now?
Boss	No, the oil we're after is called petroleum. Can you say that?
Sib	Tell us what you want!
Boss	Truth to tell, baby, all we want is to make a few little holes.
Meg	Holes? Not in the trees?
Honey and Candy	No! We love your lovely trees!
Citronella	Gasco just drills the earth.
Eva	But the earth's our mother!
Citronella	Girlie, I'm a mother!
Eva	So drill holes in yourself.

All laugh.

Citronella smiles but looks icy.

Citronella	What a witty child!
Boss	We swear to do no lasting damage. All agree we can start?
Meg	Wait! What do we get?
Tree Kids	Yeah!
Jon	We have less food 'cause your bangs have scared the animals!
Tree Kids	Yeah!

Meg	And no feast tonight!
Tree Kids	Right!
Meg	So why should we let you drill?
Tree Kids	Yes! Why, why, why?

Boss blows his whistle.

Boss	You want to know why?
Tree Kids	Yes!
Boss	Because if you let Gasco drill for oil, we promise to give you – wait for it – free food and drink for the rest of your lives!
Tree Kids	Wow!
Citronella	Think about it while our kiddies give you the facts!

All applaud and the Tree Kids exclaim in wonder as the Gas Kids open up large colourful displays of Hexie Cookies and Hexacola.

Chunky	Guys, no one hunts smelly animals for food any more!

Beefy opens a pack of Hexie Cookies.

Beefy	Isn't it smarter to open a pack of Hexies?
Tree Boys	Yes!
Honey	Girls who help Gasco needn't carry water any more!
Candy	And Hexacola's six delicious flavours come in easy-to-open cans!

Candy opens a can.

Like so!

Chunky	Accept Paw's offer and you can eat as much as you like!
Fly	There's more to life than two or three meals a day!
Beefy	Yeah, six meals a day!

All laugh.

Honey speaks to Sib.

Honey	Pity you can't see, kid!
Sib	I can see what you're doing!
Boss	Collect your tasters while you decide!
All	Hurray!

The Gas Kids hand out Hexies, cans of cola and paper Gasco caps. Citronella takes Ann to one side.

Citronella	Tell me about this wonderful flower!
Ann	Each New Year the orchid yields the oil of eternal youth. As long as we take it we'll never grow up.
Citronella	So if I had your oil I'd never age.
Boss	Enjoying your Hexies, kids?
Tree Kids	Yes!
Boss	Great! Go over there and discuss our offer. Don't mind us.
Citronella	And don't forget: you're all invited to a feast at our camp tonight!
Tree Kids	Wow!

The Gases take out a vast picnic and sit round the car eating, while the Tree Kids move away.

Sib	Gather round. Now, these folk promise free food and drink if we let 'em drill. What do you say?
Jon	I say yes, 'cause free food beats sweating through the jungle.
Rio	And I say yes, 'cause Hexacola comes in six delicious flavours.
Ann	And I say yes, 'cause they're only going to drill holes.
Eva	They're lying! They're going to build drilling rigs and refineries and gas stations and black tarmac thruways!
Rio	And what are they?
Eva	I don't know!
Rio	Well then!
Jon	I like their clothes!

All	Me too.
Jem	And their car goes like the wind. It's godlike!

He writes big letters in the air.

K-A-A! Kaa!

All	Kaa!
Sib	Gods don't stink up the world!
Ann	They say they love trees.
Fly	They're pretending! They'll kill 'em! And the woman's after the orchid!
Mac	How can you kill a forest? I say let Gasco drill!

Boss crosses the stage.

Boss	Time to decide.
Rio	We have a right to vote, Sib.
Sib	(*sighing*) Very well. Those in favour of letting our land be drilled for oil raise their hands.

All except Sib and Fly raise their hands.

Gases	Yahoo!
Sib	How many?
Fly	All but you and me.
Boss	You've made the right choice! What say we practise our singsong for the feast tonight?
Tree Kids	Yes!

Boss blows his whistle. Loud, pounding music. The Oil Gang jog in rhythmically, wearing boots, hard-hats and Gasco overalls.

Boss	Halt! Face front! Introducing your friendly oil gang:
Amis	Amis!
Beck	Beck!
Ford	Ford!
Nash	Nash!

Park	Park!
Snow	Snow!
Tate	Tate!
West	West!
Amis	Who do we serve?
Gang	(*loudly*) United Gasco: right down the line!
Boss	These kids want to learn your song. A-one, a-two, a-three!

The Gasco Gang accompany their song with karate kicks and punches.

Gasco Gang Song

Gang
We're hot-shot guys with laser eyes
And we never go off the boil.
We plough through seas and we smash through trees
As we blast through the world for oil!

When we find a field with high-grade yield
We're a supercharged machine
If you get in our way, then start to pray
'Cause when we're crossed we're mean! Yeah!

The Kids applaud as the Oil Gang put up a large poster upstage with a huge picture of a car and the words GASCO DRIVES YOUR CAR.

Beefy	Three cheers for the Gasco Gang! Hip, hip!
All	Hurray!
Beefy	Hip, hip!
All	Hurray!
Beefy	Hip, hip!
All	Hurray!
Boss	Our second number is the Hexacola song that's printed on your cans! One, two!

Kaa! 101

Song: Hexacola

All Hexacola wins out every time!
All you kids should try it!
Strawberry, cherry, grapefruit, lime:
In caffeine free and diet!

Split a six-pack with your mates
As into your car you climb.
Buy yourself a dozen crates!
Hexacola wins each time!
Hexacola wins out every time.

Boss applauds.

Boss I love it nearly as much as I love my car!

Music

Boss points to the poster.

Boss There ain't no beauty in nature like a car! Shut your eyes and you can smell it! (*Inhaling*) Ahh!

They all close their eyes and breathe in deeply.

All Ahh!
Boss Love that rubber!
All Love that rubber!
Boss Love that plastic!
All Love that plastic!
Boss Love that heavy metal!
All Love that heavy metal!
Boss Love that plastic, love that rubber, love that heavy metal!

They all sway and clap.

All Love that plastic, love that rubber, love that heavy metal! Yeah, man!
Boss Shall we seal our agreement now?
All Yes!

Boss	Raise your right hands. In return for free junk food and drink for the rest of your lives, do you solemnly agree to let us drill for oil, cut down trees ...
Gases	Thousands of trees.
Boss	Lay pipelines and cut down more trees ...
Gases	More trees.
Boss	To build gasplant and do all necessary construction work ...
Gases	Construction work!
Boss	And roads so that all can travel freely!
Tree Kids	Free travel?
Boss	Answer 'We do'.
Tree Kids	We do!

They all shake hands and embrace.

All	Hurray!
Candy	Who's coming to our place for a feast?
All	Me!
Honey	Who's for Hexies?

Shouting 'Me!' all run out.

Pounding music. The Oil Gang jog in. Calling short instructions, they rapidly remove the fireplace, cookpot, waterpot and mugs and erect two more large posters saying SITE FOR GIANT GASCO OILFIELD and GASCO APOLOGIZES FOR ANY SLIGHT INCONVENIENCE.

Amis	Fetch the truck with the drilling-rig!
All	Drilling-rig truck!

Exit Oil Gang chanting 'Drilling-rig truck!' Citronella enters and crosses to the orchid.

Citronella	Your oil holds what every woman would give the world for: the secret of eternal youth! I shall be the most powerful female on earth!

Her watch chimes twelve.

Citronella Midnight: time for your oil to flow! Open wide, my precious!

The head of the plant rises. She offers a phial.

Citronella Let the kids die! I want to live forever!

The head turns away.

Citronella Don't make me use force, baby!
    By shades of night I conjure thee,
    Yield thy magic oil to me! Now!

The plant turns and sprays her, hissing. She shrieks, trying to brush the liquid off. The plant droops. She continues to shriek. Enter Sib followed by the other Tree Kids, some holding cola cans.

Meg pushes Citronella.

Meg Shut up, you noisy old gasbag!

Citronella stops screaming and stands snuffling.

Meg Yucch! She's soaked! She's all sticky!
Sib She's stolen the orchid oil! We'll grow old and die!
Mac Rip her clothes off and get the oil out!
All Yeah!
Citronella No! Help me, please!
Sib Come with me or you'll burn.

Sib and Citronella leave the stage.

Ann She lied to us!
Jon They all lied to us!

He gestures to the posters.

Look at these!

Jem They said 'Just a few little holes in the earth', the liars!
Fly We can't trust 'em now, can we?

All No way!

The car and the Oil Gang chanting 'Drilling-rig!' can be heard.

Mac They're coming to drill! What can stop 'em?

Fly produces the cylinder.

Fly This can: watch!

Fly runs off with the cylinder. All watch.

Meg He's sneaked onto the truck!
Eva He's planted the charge!
Mac He's coming back!

Fly runs back in.

Fly Keep down! Ten, nine, eight …
All (*crouching*) Seven, six, five, four, three, two, one! Zero!

There is a pause. The car engine is getting louder. They all rise.

Rio It hasn't worked. We're finished.
Sam It's a thirty-second fuse! Down!

They all drop down again. There is an explosion and a wheel rolls onto the stage. All rise, laughing. Sib enters with Citronella, who is wearing comic underclothes and weeping loudly. All point and laugh.

Jon Where's the orchid oil?

Sib indicates her phial.

Sib Safe in here: we squeezed it out of her dress!
All Hurray!
Sib And the explosion has unblocked the well!
All Hurray!
Rio (*pointing*) Look!

All laugh as the other Gases enter with blackened faces.

Boss speaks to Citronella.

Boss I blame you!
Citronella And I blame you!
Sib Quiet! You'll have time to blame each other on the walk back.
Citronella Walk, why?
Boss Because the car was blown to bits with the drilling-rig! Let's go! One foot before the other!

The Tree Kids laugh and clap rhythmically as the Gases hobble off, moaning. They remove their Gasco caps.

Meg We'll clean up tomorrow.

Eva points to the posters.

Eva Yes, and scrap these.

Offstage, a small animal calls.

Sib Listen. The animals are coming back.

Sam drinks the last of his can of Hexacola.

Sam No more Hexacola.
Rio The trees are full of genuine fruit flavours.
All (*smiling*) Genuine fruit flavours!
Jem I loved the car. It was magic. Dead good.
Sib Our forest's even more magic. And the orchid.
Jon Hey, we never had a singsong.
Fly We can have one now. All line up! A-one, a-two, a-three:

Song: Kaa Worship

All	If you want to kill the trees, worship Kaa,
	If you want to kill the trees, worship Kaa,

The Gases and the Oil Gang enter and join in.

All	If you want to act insane
	Simply pump out acid rain
Chunky	If you haven't got a brain, worship Kaa.
All	If you want to choke the roads
Gases	Worship Kaa!
All	If you want to choke the roads
Gases	Worship Kaa!
All	Don't use bus or train or bike
	Never run or skate or hike –
Gases	We do exactly as we like and worship Kaa.

The cast all point at the audience.

All	If you want to gas the world
Gases	Worship Kaa!
All	If you want to gas the world
Gases	Worship Kaa!
All	There will be no ozone layer
	And we'll all breathe poisoned air
	If you people sitting there worship Kaa.

They repeat the last three lines becoming quieter and quieter.

The end

MUSIC
For five songs in *Kaa!*

It's a Gas

Cruis - in' 'long o' Main Street it's a gas!

Burn - in' up the thru' - way it's a gas!

Dri - vin' thru' the for - est it's a gas! An - y time an - y place

1st & 2nd verses

it's a gas! Life's a gas!

We're Gonna Be Rich!

*Spoken rap-style over the bass & chords — the 4-bar phrase covers each line of the verse, with the song 'Rich Rich Rich' at the end of each verse.

Gasco Gang Song

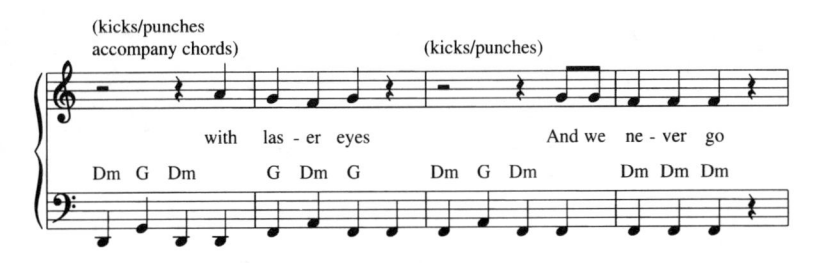

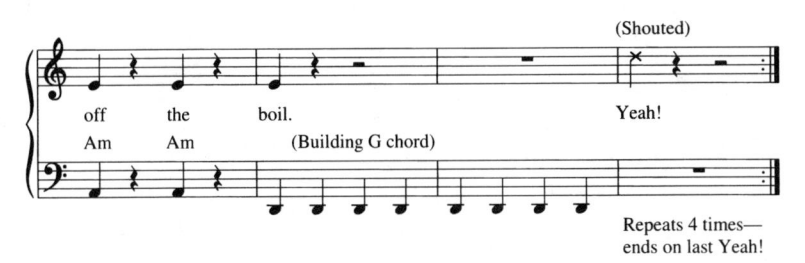

Aggressive and heavy *x 3*

We're hot shot guys

Building G chord — G — Dm G Dm

(kicks/punches accompany chords)

with las-er eyes

(kicks/punches)

And we ne-ver go

Dm G Dm — G Dm G — Dm G Dm — Dm Dm Dm

off the boil.

(Shouted) Yeah!

Am Am (Building G chord)

Repeats 4 times—ends on last Yeah!

Hexacola

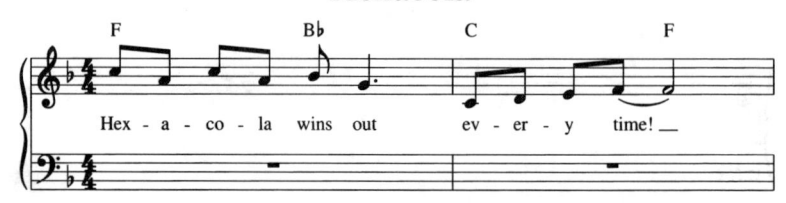

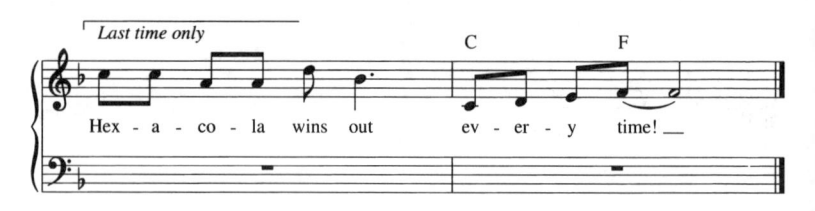

Hex-a-co-la wins out ev-er-y time!
All you kids shou-ld try it! Straw-ber-ry, cher-ry, grape-fruit, lime: in caf-feine free and di-et

Last time only
Hex-a-co-la wins out ev-er-y time!

Kaa Worship

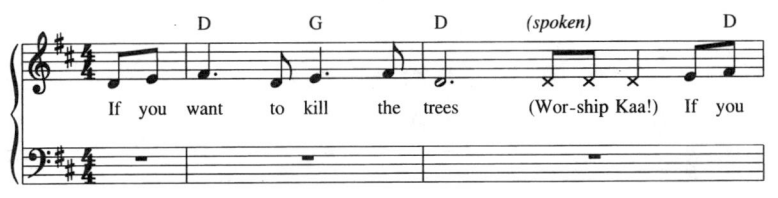

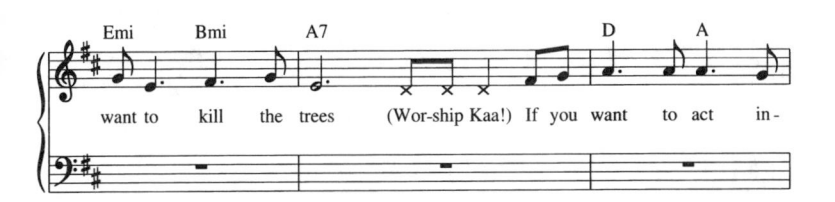

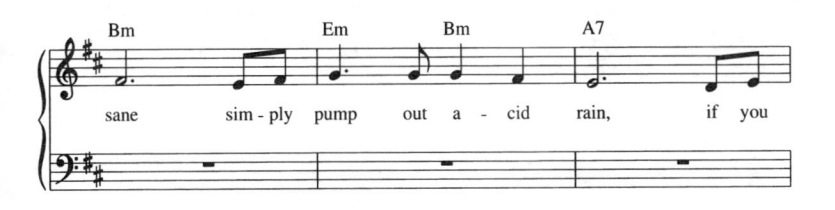

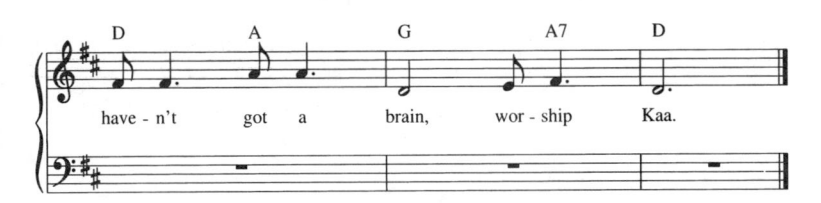

If you want to kill the trees (Wor-ship Kaa!) If you want to kill the trees (Wor-ship Kaa!) If you want to act insane simply pump out acid rain, if you haven't got a brain, wor-ship Kaa.

MUSIC

for song in *Josephine and her Sisters* on pages 21 and 25

I Got a Robe

1. I got - a robe, you got - a robe, All of God's chil - dren got - a robe; When I get to heav - en goin' to put on my robe, and wear it all ov - er God's heav - en,

heav - en, _____ heav - en, _____

Ev - 'ry - bo - dy talk - in' 'bout heav'n ain't go - in' there,

heav - en, _____ heav - en, _____ goin' to

wear it all ov - er God's heav - en. _____

QUESTIONS AND EXPLORATIONS

KEEPING TRACK

Josephine and her Sisters

1 Why do you think the author has decided to have parts of this play described by narrators instead of being fully acted out?
2 Josephine persuades some of her sisters to co-operate so that they can get money for dowries. How does the dowry system work? Would you like to pay or receive one? Why?
3 Jacob favours Joseph before his other sons, and his sons before his daughters. Have you met similar favouritism in school or at home? How does it affect the favoured and the unfavoured?
4 The author says that groups who stage this play are free to change the suggested costumes in the fashion show. Any ideas?

The Burger Bar

1 Why do the English settlers think they have the right to live in America? When they land, why do they ignore all the Americans' advice?
2 List all the things that the Americans don't understand about the English, and vice-versa.
3 Why do the Americans complain about the English killing buffalo when they themselves kill them?
4 The two groups of quarrelling men are finally reconciled by

the women in their Burger Bar. Do you like this ending? Why?

5 In real life, what has actually happened to the American Indians? What happened to the buffalo?

6 Listen to *Introducing Tobacco to Civilisation* by Bob Newhart.

The Hole in the Wall

1 Laborious suggests that the plaque on the wall should say that Hadrian put in the brainwork and they put in the real work. Do you agree that such plaques should list all the builders' names? Why?

2 Plays are usually about problems that grow to crisis-point until they have to be solved. What are the problems for the different characters in *The Hole in the Wall*? How are they solved?

3 Could the play have ended differently if Hadrian hadn't had a cold? In real life, might such a small thing have an important result? Suggest examples.

4 One reader complained that the women in *The Hole in the Wall* seem interested only in marriage. Do you think this is fair comment? Could they have something better in life to aim for? What?

Kaa!

1 Why do you think the author has made a blind girl the children's leader?

2 Chunky says 'Walkin' ain't natural'. Is he right? Should we always behave naturally?

3 Why has the author chosen 1945 as the year that Mrs Norris took the children to the forest and introduced them to the

drug from the Magic Orchid?

4 Why does the Gas Family Exploitation Company want to persuade the children to sign their agreement? What's in it for the children? Would you vote to sign it? Why?

5 In what ways do the members of the Gas Family help to bring about their own downfall?

6 After the defeat of the Gas Family, the children are preparing to resume their old way of life. Do you think they will all be satisfied with it now? Why?

7 The final song warns the audience of what will happen to the world if everyone worships Kaa. What does this mean? Is it true?

EXPLORATIONS

Activities

1 The opening of a play usually tells where and when it is set and gives some indication of what it will be about. Write the first two pages of your own play, making sure that you include all that the audience need to know about where and when it takes place. Your play can be an original idea or based on a story you have read or on a historical event. Try also to indicate who the main characters are and what the play will be about. Read it to the rest of the class. Can the audience follow what's happening from what you have written without further explanation?

2 How many modern references can you find in the three plays set in the past? Write your own version of a nursery rhyme or a traditional story, including modern inventions (e.g. a mobile phone, a gun, a helicopter, an insect spray, a microwave, a tumbledrier).

Questions and Explorations

3 Split into small groups. In about 10 minutes, all go through the same play making a list of all the properties – things like letters, weapons, utensils, money, food and drink – used in the play. (Include everything except scenery, furniture and costumes.) Score 1 point for a prop listed by more than one other team, 2 for a prop listed by only one other team, and 3 for anything that only your team has found.

4 Sound effects (usually on tape) are all the sounds in a play or a film not produced by the actors, such as thunder, rain, traffic, telephones and animals. List all the sound effects mentioned in these plays. Now add one other effect for each play that you think would help the audience believe in the setting.

5 You can vary the lighting in a stage production to make a performance more dramatic. You can make the overall lighting brighter or dimmer, you can alter the colour and you can use spotlights to highlight groups or individual characters.

Work through either *Kaa!* or *Josephine and her Sisters* to make a 'lighting script'. Say when you would alter the lighting to make it brighter or dimmer, when you would highlight certain characters, etc.

6 Choose a group of characters from any of the plays and sketch or describe their costumes.

7 Either draw a ground-plan of the setting of one of these plays or draw the scene as the audience would see it.

8 The following jumbled words are the minimum eight pieces of information which all advertising of public performances should contain: (a) cittek spreic, (b) uneev, (c) letti, (d) stead, (e) meti, (f) trapwhigly, (g) ginkoob, (h) mypacno. First unjumble them, then design a poster for the performance of a play. Would a member of the public be able to book a seat from the information that you have included?

Drama

1 Characters on stage who are excited will often, as in life, raise their voices even louder than usual. Especially when two groups are involved, each speech may be louder than the previous one. Try building a crescendo in each of the following extracts:

   a *'Josephine and her Sisters'* Page 6, from 'I don't care if I never see ...' to 'Oh, yes, it does!'

   b *'Josephine and her Sisters'* Page 17, from 'Esther and Judith, two young men have asked to marry you' to 'Quiet!!'

   c *'The Burger Bar'* Page 38, from 'What was that noise?' to 'We told them, but they won't listen!'

   d *'The Burger Bar'* Page 40, from 'You surely don't live in tents ... ?' to 'Sorry we spoke!'

   e *'The Hole in the Wall'* Page 62, from 'Erm, there's just one problem, Rosie' to 'Did we listen?' 'No!'

   f *'The Hole in the Wall'* Page 78, from 'Whisht, man!' to 'And we're married to you! Hurray!' 'Hurray!'

   g *'Kaa!'* Page 96, from 'We swear to do no lasting damage' to 'Why, why, why?'

   h *'Kaa!'* Page 101, from 'Love that rubber' to 'Yeah, man!'

2 In a big acting space, actors may need to make big gestures to show their feelings or make their meaning clear. Try this exercise:

   a All face the speaker, who asks 'Where is it?' All answer: 'Over there' accompanied by a nod of the head. The speaker repeats the question louder and receives the same reply, but louder and with a bigger gesture (pointing with a hitch-hiker's thumb). Now the speaker shouts 'Where is it?' and the group shout 'Over there!' pointing with outstretched arms.

b The speaker repeats the question, but this time the group reply 'We don't know', beginning with a slight shrug and making a bigger gesture with each repetition of their reply.

c The speaker says 'Follow me!' three times. The group reply 'No!', each time louder and with a bigger gesture.

d Three times the speaker asks 'Who are the greatest?' The group reply 'We are!'

3 Now perform the following with appropriate volume and gestures:

a *'Josephine'* Page 9: 'Zing, Zing, Zing'.

b *'Josephine'* Page 19: 'Meanwhile the boys were in Egypt'.

c *'The Burger Bar'* Page 50: from 'Friends, do not listen ...' to 'Hold it! Hold it!'.

d *'The Hole in the Wall'* Page 81: 'The Squaddies are Marching Home'.

e *'Kaa!'* Page 88: 'It's a Gas'.

f *'Kaa!'* Page 100: 'The Gasco Gang Song'.

GLOSSARY: JOSEPHINE

Page

15	*brooded*	thought sadly
3	*Canaan*	country in the Middle East in Biblical times
12	*colourfast*	dye that does not come out in the wash
15	*dire*	dreadful
16	*dowry*	money given by a bride's parents to her new husband
15	*drought*	lack of rain
24	*ethnic*	belonging to a particular race
15	*hasten*	hurry
20	*hostage*	someone held against their will until some condition is fulfilled
6	*mascot*	something or someone believed to bring good luck
15	*misted*	unclear, foggy
14	*mourning*	feeling very sad because someone has died
20	*psyched*	mentally prepared
20	*scorching*	extremely hot
10	*spindle*	weighted rod used to spin wool
5	*sub*	substitute
20	*tootsies*	feet
19	*woe*	sorrow

GLOSSARY: THE BURGER BAR

Page

42	*avowed*	declared
34	*barbaric*	rough, uncivilized
29	*bison*	large cattle that used to roam wild on the American prairies
29	*boulder*	large rock
37	*buffalo*	British name for the bison
50	*bugle*	musical instrument similar to a trumpet
45	*carcass*	dead body of an animal
36	*Cheyenne*	American Indian tribe
42	*constancy*	faithfulness
44	*cool smoke*	mild tobacco
50	*crescendo*	music or other noise that gradually gets louder
44	*cured*	preserved by drying
47	*deformed*	mis-shapen
36	*dud*	useless
38	*dominion*	control
36	*exotic*	strange or unusual
36	*fabled*	legendary, famous
38	*fowl*	birds
38	*Hallelujah!*	Praise the Lord!
42	*intent*	intention, plan
35	*lepers*	people with leprosy, which altered the way they looked
51	*maize*	corn on the cob
36	*monotonous*	boring, unchanging
33	*Pastor*	church minister

42	*pilgrim*	somebody who makes a journey to visit a holy place, a devout person
31	*poppadums*	thin, crisp Indian bread
29	*prairie*	large area of grassland without any trees
49	*prophet*	somebody who claims to be able to see what will happen in the future
42	*relent*	to give in, to give up
36	*scalping*	killing
41	*sinews*	tough threads in an animal's limbs
36	*Sioux*	American Indian tribe
35	*squaw*	American Indian woman
29	*supplication*	prayer
29	*tepee*	conical tent made of skins, wigwam
42	*valiant*	brave
38	*vermin*	harmful animals
30	*weevils*	small grubs that get into food, especially on ships
40	*wigwam*	conical tent made of skins, tepee

GLOSSARY: THE HOLE IN THE WALL

Page

78	*barbarians*	uncivilized people
57	*Centurion*	officer in the Roman army
63	*chariots*	Roman vehicles
61	*civvy*	civilian, not uniform
78	*distilled*	strengthened by removing the water by distillation
78	*dram*	drink
71	*éclat*	splendour
76	*ken*	know
76	*kilt*	pleated tartan skirt worn by some Scottish men
76	*lassies*	girls
62	*pension*	money paid to people after they stop work
66	*plaque*	plate put up to commemorate something
77	*Saturn's day*	Saturday
71	*Schwarzenegger*	muscular film actor
65	*scroll*	roll of parchment or paper
76	*skean-dhu*	short knife worn in the right sock by men in Highland dress
76	*sporran*	pouch or purse worn in front of a kilt
81	*squaddy*	soldier
59	*surveyor's wheel*	instrument used to measure distance
80	*tams*	soft woollen Scottish caps, like berets
71	*tartan trews*	trousers in a Scottish tartan or check
72	*tunic*	loose garment that comes to the hip or knees

GLOSSARY: KAA!

Page		
106	*acid rain*	rain which has acid in it. The acid comes from pollution, and the acid rain damages the environment.
91	*black tarmac thruways*	wide roads built to carry heavy vehicles
91	*closet*	wardrobe
103	*conjure*	beg or beseech
89	*cookies*	biscuits
91	*drilling rig*	machinery for digging an oil well
98	*eternal*	everlasting
96	*exploitation*	taking advantage of something selfishly
106	*insane*	very foolish, crazy
88	*khaki*	yellowy brown colour
100	*laser*	very penetrating beam of light
88	*logo*	badge or symbol to advertise a brand name or organization
91	*mega-rich*	extremely rich
106	*ozone layer*	layer in the atmosphere that is destroyed by pollution
89	*petroleum*	oil as it is found underground, before it is processed
87	*phial*	small bottle
91	*refinery*	place where oil is processed
89	*seismograph*	instrument that measures underground shock waves, used in finding oil
102	*solemnly*	seriously, thoughtfully
98	*tasters*	samples to taste